S0-AZU-143

The Exploratorium Guide to Scale and Structure

The Exploratorium Guide to Scale and Structure

Activities for the Elementary Classroom

Barry Kluger-Bell
and the School in the Exploratorium

Heinemann • Portsmouth, NH

Heinemann
A division of Reed Elsevier Inc.
361 Hanover Street
Portsmouth, NH 03801-3912

Offices and agents throughout the world

© 1995 by the Exploratorium

All rights reserved. No part of this book except for Appendixes C and D (pp. 191–198) may be reproduced in any form or by any electronic or mechanical means, including information storage and retrieval systems, without permission in writing from the publisher, except by a reviewer, who may quote brief passages in a review.

Every effort has been made to contact the copyright holders for permission to reprint borrowed material where necessary. We regret any oversights that may have occurred and would be happy to rectify them in future printings of this work.

The author and publisher wish to thank those who have generously given permission to reprint borrowed material:

Excerpt from *Why Buildings Stand Up* by Mario Salvadori. © 1980. Reprinted by permission of W. W. Norton & Company.

Excerpt from *On Size and Life* by McMahon and Bonner. © 1983 by Thomas A. McMahon and John Tyler Bonner. Reprinted by permission of W. H. Freeman and Company.

This book is based upon work supported by the National Science Foundation under Grant No. ES1-9153837.

Any opinions, findings, and conclusions or recommendations expressed in this material are those of the authors and do not necessarily reflect the views of the National Science Foundation.

Library of Congress Cataloging-in-Publication Data
Kluger-Bell, Barry.
    The Exploratorium guide to scale and structure : activities for the elementary classroom / Barry Kluger-Bell and the School in the Exploratorium.
        p.   cm.
    Includes bibliographical references.
    ISBN 0-435-08372-4 (alk. paper)
    1. Science—Study and teaching (Elementary) 2. Structural engineering—Study and teaching (Elementary) 3. Education, Elementary—Activity programs.   I. School in the Exploratorium (San Francisco, Calif.) II. Title.
    LB1585.K57   1995
    372.3'58—dc20
                                                                95-8967
                                                                CIP

Editor: Leigh Peake
Production: Vicki Kasabian
Text and cover design: Jenny Jensen Greenleaf

Printed in the United States of America on acid-free paper
99 98 97 96 95 VG 1 2 3 4 5

printed on
recycled paper

Contents

Acknowledgments

At the Exploratorium, no one works alone. Without the help of many members of the Exploratorium staff and friends of the Exploratorium, this book would never have reached its current form.

The most important contributions came from teachers, particularly the Scale and Structure working group, which helped develop and test these activities in the classroom. These teachers are Linda Block, Angela Campbell, Marina Chiappellone, Kathie Fischer, Phil Hicks, Thea Mills, Stephanie Ortega-Kennison, Caroline Satoda, and Dee Uyeda. Teachers Leah Brown, Tine Clinton, and Julia Marrero contributed photographs of students in action and examples of students' work. And many teachers, too numerous to list, participated in the School in the Exploratorium workshops in which these materials were developed and tested.

This book owes much to the School in the Exploratorium program and its unique approach to investigation. School in the Exploratorium artists Bobbi Cook-Bedell and Daniel DiPierro and artist coordinator Mildred Howard added much to the material. I'd also like to acknowledge the contributions of Science Resource Teacher Cappy Greene and School in the Exploratorium Program Director Lynn Rankin, as well as the help of School in the Exploratorium program assistants Macall Gordon and Nancy Fuluso.

Bronwyn Bevan deserves special credit for taking the disparate elements and constructing a unified whole. My thanks for her dedicated writing and editing.

Other members of the Exploratorium staff contributed time and effort to making this book possible. Pat Murphy, Kurt Feichtmeir, and Rob Semper helped manage the transformation of the rough manuscript to its final form. Publications Assistant Megan Bury bailed me out with assistance in scanning images at the eleventh hour.

Finally, special thanks to Exploratorium Director Goéry Delacôte for his steadfast support of this project and to David and Francis Hawkins for contributing to my interest in science education and particularly the topic of Scale and Structure.

—Barry Kluger-Bell

Introduction

Children love to build. Almost as soon as they can manipulate objects, they begin to put them on top of one another. They move on to build with blocks, cardboard boxes, and the pillows from your favorite sofa. In a world full of structures, they have encountered many houses, bridges, skyscrapers, bees' nests, and tree branches. They therefore come to the topic of Scale and Structure with a wealth of ideas and full of questions. The world around us provides hundreds of starting points for exploring this topic, including both natural and human-made structures. In this book, we use children's love of building and buildings to explore many of the physical principles of structure.

Children are also fascinated with the world of the big and the small. From dollhouses and miniature cars to the giants of cartoons and movies, the idea of life in the world of the tiny and the large seems to grab a child's attention. We connect with this interest using activities that have children build on different scales. Through this process, you and your students will experience how changing the scale of a structure affects the nature (the strength, the stability, and the design) of the structure itself.

The relationship between scale and structure is found throughout the disciplines. It can be seen when you look at how the expansive Golden Gate Bridge differs from a smaller plank crossing a creek, how giant redwoods differ from smaller maples, and why elephant legs are proportionately thicker than the legs of mice. Many structural differences in the world can be explained purely in terms of scale change.

The activities in this book will help your students to develop a feeling for and an understanding of structure and its change with scale change. The book is designed as a guide and set of activities for third- through eighth-grade teachers who would like to explore this realm with their students. We have had great fun and learned quite a lot while developing it. We hope you enjoy using it too.

Where did this book come from?

The Exploratorium is a museum where people make discoveries for themselves. The museum has over 670 exhibits, and all of them run on curiosity. You don't just look at these exhibits, you play with them—turning knobs, pushing buttons, peering through lenses, and rewiring electrical circuits. The Exploratorium is a public laboratory where people of all ages can experiment with scientific demonstrations, artwork, experiments, and perceptual puzzles.

The goal of the School in the Exploratorium program is to inspire and support fundamental change in the way that science is taught in the elementary school classroom. For more than two decades, this program has used the Exploratorium as a laboratory in its work with hundreds of local K–5 educators.

Intensive summer institutes and an ongoing series of weekend and after-school workshops focus on working with teachers to develop ways to move classroom teaching from textbook-based instruction to student-centered investigation and discovery. The activities and curricula designed for these workshops (and later implemented in the K–5 classrooms) integrate science and art in hands-on investigations of natural phenomena.

Three years ago—and partly in response to the recently issued California State Science Framework that emphasized thematic-based teaching—a group consisting of two artists, a physicist, and seven classroom teachers came together to develop teaching materials around the theme of Scale and Structure. The theme provided a rich opportunity to explore both science and art, as the fundamentals of both physical structure and aesthetic architectural design were inherently integrated in almost every investigation of the phenomena. The activities were tested in many teacher workshops and even more in K–5 classrooms. Building on students' natural curiosity and love of building, they explore some of the most fundamental physics concepts involved in construction and scaling. The resulting set of activities is different from those contained in the many good building books and curricula on structure (listed in Appendix B) in that it emphasize *scale* and its effects on structure.

When we started this project we did not set out to produce a book. However, the response to the material by both students and teachers has been so positive that we now want to share the ideas with more of our colleagues.

What we present here is not a book designed to "teach the theme" of Scale and Structure, but the results of a series of explorations around the big question, *How do physical-mechanical structures change with changes in scale?* Three central conceptual areas emerged when we investigated that big question: the Physics and Engineering of Structure, the Mathematics of Scale, and the Effects of Scale on Structure. We have organized the activities accordingly.

How can you use this book?

This book should be considered as a collection of starting points that provide endless opportunities for sustained investigations and experimentation The activities explore a set of phenomena using different materials and different approaches, thus allowing students to develop a deep understanding of the phenomena over time. How you select and order these activities depends on the goals you set for yourself and your class. We encourage you to personalize, to build upon, and to create new activities to suit your own philosophy and style of teaching.

The development and writing of this book began with inquiry-based activities and ended with explanations of the concepts encountered in those activities. The traditional method of teaching consists of a lecture and then a lab designed to demonstrate what has been covered by the lecture. At the Exploratorium, we encourage visitors, teachers, and students to experiment and observe in the "lab" first, and then use their observations to create models of how the world works. Along the way, they question, test, and carefully consider the phenomena they encounter during construction. In recording their observations and findings as a class, patterns and consistencies emerge that lead naturally to the existence of fundamental concepts. This open-ended, student-directed approach to learning leads students to seek the answers rather than receive them.

The Exploratorium approach to teaching and learning not only encourages students to seek out answers through experimentation but it also asks teachers to do the same. Teachers who come to the School in the Exploratorium's workshops find themselves put in the role of experimenters rather than note-takers. Teachers are encouraged to explore with their students, learning through the process of experimentation. Rather than being an expert with all of the answers, the teacher becomes a person who can guide the learning process and help students make discoveries along the way.

As you read the book and think about the activities, keep in mind that you don't need to know all of the answers before you begin. A willingness to explore and experiment will, in the long run, get you farther than a degree in physics or an understanding of every technical term would.

How does this book relate to the Scale and Structure theme?

Recently, the idea of thematic instruction in science has taken a strong foothold nationwide. Since its initial introduction in the AAAS: Project 2061 document, *Science for All Americans,*[1] the idea has appeared in a number of state science frameworks. The idea of "themes" as referenced in the frameworks is different and broader than the traditional idea of making whales or dinosaurs a classroom theme for the year. Framework themes are not subject-oriented, but concept-oriented. The framework themes are meant to "link the theoretical structures of the various scientific disciplines and show how they are logically parallel and cohesive."[2] The power of themes is based on an idea that scientists use all of the time: that "basic concepts in one field can be transferred by connection or analogy to another field."[3]

Themes are not meant to be *what* you teach, but *how* you teach. Thematic teaching is an approach that moves science teaching from its current emphasis on isolated details to an emphasis on the important ideas in science and the connections between them.

The theme of Scale and Structure (or simply Scale) appears in many state science frameworks and projects of national importance.[4] The major idea of this theme is that a change in scale will affect the nature of a given structure—you cannot grow or shrink an object without taking into account how the new scale will adversely or favorably affect the integrity of your structure.

This is true for a wide range of disciplines and subdisciplines. In engineering, if you want to "grow" a tower from 10 feet tall to 100 feet tall, you will need to broaden the base in order to avoid having the tower topple over (for an explanation, see center-of-mass in the overview of the *Physics and Engineering of Structure* section). In biology, if you "shrink" a bird from ostrich-size to sparrow-size, you will increase the surface-area-to-volume ratio, causing the smaller bird to lose more heat through its proportionately larger surface area. The small bird will need to eat constantly to replace the lost heat/energy (see the *Beyond This Book* section for more details). The effects of scale on structure show up in ecological, behavioral, chemical, and geological structures, among others. In physics, structural effects that depend on scale show up in thermodynamics, electricity, and mechanics as well as in the structure of matter (i.e., atoms at small scale and stars at larger scale).

This book covers a narrow slice of the range of disciplines listed above. However, if students can get the big idea of how scale affects structure, they will have a "basic concept" that "can be transferred by connection or analogy to another field." Once you understand the idea of the effect of scale on structure in this narrow context, you are ready to begin to spot it in other contexts and, eventually, to see it as a broad theme.

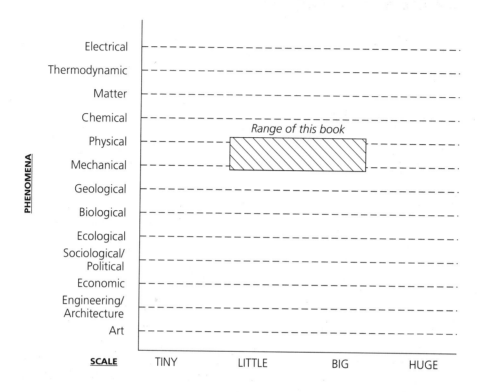

Notes

1. *Science for All Americans*, New York: Oxford University Press, 1990.

2. *Science Framework for California Public Schools,* Sacramento, Calif.: California Department of Education, 1990, 26.

3. *Ibid.,* 28.

4. E.g., AAAS: Project 2061 (*Science for All Americans*), *The National Assessment of Educational Progress,* and the National Science Teachers Association Scope, Sequence, and Coordination Project.

Teaching Scale and Structure

Nuts and Bolts

In preparing for and implementing a scale and structure unit, there are several important basics to keep in mind.

Space

◆ Many of these activities require special areas or space considerations. During the investigations, you will often need substantial *building space.* For activities that extend over more than one session, you will need to establish *storage space* for the constructions. Finally, you might want to think about *display space* for the finished products.

Time

◆ Building often takes more time than you think it will. Give yourself and your students lots of time for all the elements of each activity. Students will need time to build, discuss, and clean up. It is critical that students have time to discuss ideas before, during, and after the activities.

◆ Include ample time for initial exploration of the materials themselves.

◆ As in all activities, groups or individuals work at a variety of paces. Be prepared with parallel alternative activities for those who may finish early. See the *Extensions* at the end of most activities for some suggestions.

Talking and Writing

Before starting an activity, talking about the topic and helping students make connections to their own experiences and prior knowledge is essential. Writing, recording observations, and discussion help children to construct their own understanding out of these activities. Here are some ideas to help you get started.

◆ Write with your students and do whole-group modeling and "think-alouds" before expecting students to work independently.

◆ Consider what you want students to write on or in (e.g., record sheet, notebook, learning log, journal), when you want them to write (e.g., before, during, and/or after an activity), how you respond to student writing, and how students can share their writing.

◆ To facilitate and support student thinking and learning, vary the purpose, form, and audience of the writing. Descriptive writing, narrative writing, recording steps in a process, persuasive writing, poetry, fiction, letters, cross-grade or buddy journals as well as "lab sheets" call for very different kinds of responses that foster a broad base of thinking upon which student understanding is built.

◆ Consistently ask yourself, "How does this writing foster student learning?"

Unit Planning

There are many possible pathways through this material. These pathways emphasize different concepts or work better with certain teaching and learning styles. Whichever path you choose, the activities selected and the order in which they are done need to fit into a conceptual context and fit with your teaching style and your students' learning levels and styles. The optimal choice of activities, modifications of activities, and order in which you do them can only be determined by you, the teacher. Things to consider as you design your work are presented below.

Goals for the Unit

When you design your scale and structure unit you will have to determine which of the many possible specific goals are most important to you. For instance, if you put a good deal of emphasis on balance, you may set some operational goals for student understanding such as:

◆ Students will know how to balance two blocks on one side of a balance board with one block on the other side, or

◆ Students will demonstrate their knowledge that when a structure's center-of-mass is lower, the stability is greater.

Listed below are more general goals that we have found to be important in implementing the scale and structure unit.

◆ Students will develop an increased awareness of and an interest and operational understanding of torques and forces, weight, structural properties of materials, stability, and balance. By operational, we mean that students show their understanding through their interaction with the materials.

◆ Students will observe that lengths, areas, and volumes change differently as you scale up or down; they will begin to see a connection between these differences and the effects of scale change on structure.

◆ Students will demonstrate an understanding of the principle that as you scale up or down, physical properties change at very different rates and that at different scales materials behave differently.

◆ Students will recognize and value their growing competence as builders.

◆ Students will develop enhanced facility, clarity, and sophistication in oral and written communication of their ideas, understandings, and questions about scale and structure.

◆ Students will begin to recognize "structural elements" and the effects of scale in many different contexts, both inside and outside the classroom. They will talk about structures and structural elements and relate them to the "outside world." They will "see more" and look at their world/environment with a broader and deeper perspective.

◆ Students will build an operational and experiential foundation for broader conceptual understandings of structure and scale. Manifestations of these understandings may not appear until much later in their intellectual development. Eventually, students can begin to synthesize and generalize their understandings from the perspective of physics and engineering to that of biology, sociology/anthropology, and other areas. For example, in biology they may look for scale-related differences between insects and elephants, and in sociology/anthropology they may look for scale-related differences between small groups and crowds.

Selecting Activities

When you put together your unit you will be selecting activities from this and other references, modifying activities and probably inventing new activities. In our work we have found the following ideas important to keep in mind:

◆ Use accessible, familiar manipulative materials.

◆ Leave plenty of time for initial explorations of the materials themselves.

◆ Use inherently weak materials—things that are barely up to the task—so that there are difficulties from the start, and problem solving occurs throughout the experience.

◆ Set well-defined limits on materials and connectors (both types and amounts) so that there is some common ground to student work.

◆ Ensure that the activities add to students' conceptual understanding. Ask yourself, Does this activity help students make meaning of this unit?

◆ Connect the activities with student observations and experiences outside the classroom.

◆ Balance exploratory, challenge/competitive, and directed activities. It is easy to make too many of the activities challenges or competitions. In order to avoid some of the competitiveness, establish a variety of measures of success such as most efficient, strongest, highest, longest, most spectacular, lightest, most imaginative, etc.

◆ Include elements of "fair testing" in many activities. For example, when building a tower that will hold weight, students want to know whose tower will hold the most weight. For this competition to be "fair," they want everyone to follow the same rules. They may suggest that all weights be hung from a point on the tower two feet up. In doing this, students are recognizing that both the weight and the position of the weight may be important "variables" in this experiment. In order to get a "fair" test, they recognize that the variable of position of the weight must stay the same while they vary the amount of weight hanging on the tower. This is a good step in learning to recognize and isolate variables.

The organization and processes of the activities are also important. We have found the following to be important considerations:

◆ Introduce activities with student discussion of related experiences or knowledge that they bring to the work. For instance, when doing *Straws and Pins—Building Up* have students talk about tall buildings and towers that they have seen.

◆ Include students in discussions and decisions concerning building parameters and structural testing.

◆ Adapt group size to your circumstances, taking into account the time, materials, and adult assistance available to you.

- Have students make predictions to help determine and frame discoveries.

- Use guiding questions to focus and encourage discoveries, discussion, and writing.

- Have students write, keep records, and verbally process what they are doing and discovering.

- Some activities can best be introduced as learning centers. These learning centers are activity areas where a small group of students can work relatively independently with a set of materials. For example, activities in *Balancing Acts* work well when introduced as centers. This gives students a chance to be introduced to phenomena through several different experiences in close proximity. Ongoing learning centers give students an opportunity to continue to pursue a question or experiment and refine their understanding. Centers can be modified by adding or substituting different materials, or new centers can replace old ones as the unit progresses.

- Processing is critical to deeper learning. Vary the processing experience among individual, pair, small group, and whole-class discussion. Adequate processing time is critical for students to move from isolated experiences to broader generalizations.

Constructivist Underpinnings

Underlying the design of these activities, and this discussion of unit planning, is the belief that students come to this work with a set of experiences and knowledge that will serve as their starting points. Student work in the classroom must be connected with this prior knowledge and extracurricular experience if the work is to influence their understanding of the world. Some of the classroom work can reinforce student beliefs. Other experiences will challenge previously held notions. But this cannot happen if "school learning" is isolated from out-of-school experience. It is our responsibility as teachers to help students to integrate their disparate experiences of the subject at hand.

There are a number of important elements that school experiences must contain if they are to influence students' mental models of the phenomena.

- Students must engage in activities that illuminate central concepts in multiple contexts. A single illustration of an idea is not enough.

- The activities must give students the latitude to raise their own questions and to try to find answers firsthand from materials.

- Students must be given encouragement and time to process their experiences in a number of ways (e.g., writing, drawing, and discussing).

- Students must have a chance to share ideas and discoveries, since part of building understanding happens by interacting with others.

- Students must be assisted in generating their own models of the phenomena and prompted to compare their models with those of their fellow students and with the "accepted" models. In this process, student ideas must be honored and alternatives argued logically from the evidence available.

These elements make the school experience an effective means of enhancing the construction of understanding by students.

We share the vision of the "constructivist" classroom articulated by Bernard Farges of the San Francisco Unified School District:

> In a "constructivist" classroom, students are afforded numerous opportunities to explore phenomena and ideas, conjecture, share hypotheses with others, and revise their original thinking. Students are not given knowledge, but instead they are given the opportunity to make sense of their own world. They learn through reflection and resolution of cognitive conflict and superseding earlier incomplete levels of understanding. . . . The key tenet of the constructivist approach is that people learn by actively constructing knowledge, weighing new information against their previous understanding, thinking about and working through discrepancies (on their own and with others), and coming to a new understanding.

Cross-Curricular Work

The topic of Scale and Structure leads to a very natural mix of curriculum areas. The structure of houses can lead to the study of heating, lighting, and furnishing. Bridges can lead to the study of traffic, great bridges of the world, and the history of the people who built them. Sculpture and architecture are also naturally connected. Living things can also be included in your unit. Compare the rigidity of tree trunks with the flexibility of grass, and observe animal constructions, such as spiderwebs and honeycombs.

Try these activities along with your class, and have fun with your unit.

A Sample Unit for Fifth Grade

The following unit example is not meant to be proscriptive or prescriptive. The big ideas which it is designed to develop in student understanding have led to the choice of activities and the order in which they are presented. You may have very different goals, or "big ideas," which you wish to have your unit lead to. The text in italics explains some of the thinking behind the choices of activities. When you design your own unit, consider it to be a "rough blueprint" which will evolve over time as you see where the activities lead the students and yourself. Be flexible.

What's the Big Idea?

This sample unit is a major focus for science in a classroom and can be carried out over a period of about three months. In planning this particular unit, we have decided to focus on building up and establishing a base for the understanding of scale and the effects of scale. The big ideas that we are aiming at are listed below. We may be aiming a little high, but we would rather do that than underestimate the students. We do not expect our fifth graders to develop a complete understanding of the connection between the mathematics of scaling and physical scale effects, but they are intellectually mature enough to recognize that there is a connection. This recognition will lay a foundation for a more complete understanding to be developed in later years. This unit has three big ideas.

◆ *A structure's design must effectively counterbalance the natural forces that tend to pull it down.* Whether a structure stands or collapses depends on the outcome of the "battle" between the forces pulling it down (gravity/weight) versus those holding it up (strength of material, how materials are combined, and how individual pieces are joined). The concepts of forces, torques, stability, center-of-mass, tension, and compression are integral to understanding how this battle unfolds.

♦ *Different dimensions scale at different rates.* As you scale up or down, areas (and things that depend on area, like strength) and volumes (and things that depend on volume, like weight) grow or shrink at very different rates.

♦ *Scale affects structure.* The physical structure of things in the world may differ purely because of a change in scale.

Before Beginning the Unit

♦ Establish a "building area" where students can explore building with a variety of materials (see the *General Building* activity).

♦ Many activities assume student familiarity and proficiency at working in groups. Establish student experience in this area before starting the unit. (For more information, see *Classroom Management* below and the endnotes.)

♦ Start the unit with a neighborhood field trip to look at tall buildings, church spires, pylons for high-voltage wires, and tall trees. Also, bring in and have students bring in pictures of remarkable structures, both natural and man-made. Since this unit's building focus is building up, connection to these "real-world" tall structures makes a great start.

♦ Gather artwork, or photos of and literature about artwork, to share with students throughout the unit. This will help with the interdisciplinary work done during the unit.

Activities

The unit continues with the following activities done in the order listed:

1 Straws and Pins—Building Up

2 Toothpicks and Clay

3 Introduction to Cubes

4 Growing Cubes

5 Cones and Scale

6 Clay Towers

7 Fruit and Vegetable Area

8 Scaled Newspaper Structures (medium scale)

9 Shrinking Cubes

10 Scaled Newspaper Structures (small scale, large scale)

11 Water Drop Pennies and Water Domes

12 Floating Pins and Paper Clips

13 Garden Poles and Skewers—Building Up

14 Building Up—Assessment

15 *Powers of Ten* Video and Discussion of Scale

Below are explanations of why these particular activities were selected.

We have chosen to begin this unit with two building-up activities. Building activities like these are very engaging, providing a good momentum to propel students into the unit. We also want students to encounter the basic principles of structure early in the unit. We choose activities that use weak materials so that these principals become evident early in the building process. We started with two similar activities that use very different materials so that students see these principles in multiple contexts and learn to abstract the general principles from the specific experience.

Straws and Pins—Building Up

This is a great activity to start with after the neighborhood field trip and structure pictures. All of the conceptual elements of structure that we want students to deal with are encountered in this activity. Work in this activity will take place over two days.

Toothpicks and Clay

This activity illustrates many of the same principles and ideas as the above activity, but uses different materials. It also facilitates student focus on underlying structural concepts, and helps students to be more proficient builders. The scale is similar to the first activity, providing some grounding before trying different scales.

Given the emphasis that we have chosen for this unit, we want to get students to look at the mathematical aspects early in the unit. The following activity gives them a start.

Introduction to Cubes

This activity is a nice transition from pure building to some of the mathematical aspects of the topic. The activity starts out with building using the new medium of sugar cubes. It ends by having students look at lengths, areas, and volumes of the things that they have built.

The next two activities push the math of scale aspects even further, while maintaining a strong connection with the physical processes of building.

Growing Cubes

This activity illustrates the mathematical relationships of length, area, and volume at different scales. Understanding this basic concept provides a foundation for understanding the effect of scale on structure. Cubes provide a good starting point for investigating this relationship, since they are easily measured and counted and the structure is easy to build.

Cones and Scale

It is a good idea to provide more than one geometric shape for students to observe and experience the relationship between length, area, and volume at different scales. In the previous activity, students worked with cubes. To increase the scale of a cube you must increase the length, width, and height. It is not obvious that scale increases in other shapes will result in the same mathematical relationships of length, area, and volume. In this activity, students build cones, enlarging them by increasing the diameter of the circle from which the cone is built. Finding that the same mathematical relationships of length, area, and volume exist with cones as with cubes as the scale changes provides students with evidence that this pattern is universal.

After spending a good deal of time on these mathematical aspects of the unit, it is important to reconnect with building.

Clay Towers

This activity gives students a very different material with which to build towers. It helps students see that the lower layers of the tower must support the upper layers. Given the emphasis of this unit, we ask students how tall they could build with twice as much clay or with half as much clay, and then have them test their predictions. This can lead to a discussion about how scale affects a structure's design.

Before beginning activities that deal more directly with the physical effects of changing scale, we want students to get additional experience with the mathematics of scale. The following activity takes the results found with cubes and cones and expands them to real-world objects.

Fruit and Vegetable Area

Presenting this activity at this point in the unit, we would use pairs of potatoes, oranges, or other fruits or vegetables of similar shapes but different size. For instance, students might work with apples 2 inches and 4 inches in diameter (not an apple and a carrot) to facilitate their observations and measurements of how the areas and volumes scale up and down with size changes.

Scaled Newspaper Structures (medium scale)

This activity takes a new material, newspaper, which is weak and full of problem-solving opportunities, and allows students to extend and expand what they've learned to a new area. This activity as written entails building on three different scales. We start with the medium size of the three scales, so students can focus on the structural aspects of their work before turning their attention to what happens with scale change.

Before building with newspaper on a smaller scale, we want students to have some explicit experience with scaling down. Up to this point, all of the mathematics of scale activities have dealt with increasing sizes. The mathematical patterns are the same when you shrink in scale. However, students will need explicit experience dealing with reducing scale, such as that provided in the following activity, if they are to understand the patterns of reduced scale.

Shrinking Cubes

This activity illustrates the mathematical patterns that emerge when reducing length, area, and volume as you scale down. By slicing clay cubes, students can get direct experience of the fact that area is reduced faster than length and that volume is reduced even faster. This provides important clues in understanding the reduced-scale building found in the next activity.

Scaled Newspaper Structures (small scale, large scale)

We now return to newspaper building by doing the small-scale *Scaled Newspaper Structures* activity. Students get direct, concrete experience of the differences in working with the same material but at a smaller scale. The shift to the large-scale *Scaled Newspaper Structures* activity after working on a small scale is dramatic. Students find that it is almost like working with a different material. Reference to their previous experiences with cubes, cones, and tower building will help them to understand what is happening at the different scales.

In the following water activities, students will observe some additional examples of scale effects. These activities provide a start for extending students' nascent understanding of scale effects to a wider realm.

Water Drop Pennies and Water Domes

These activities provide direct, simple experiences of the effect of scale on structure. In the first, students are given an introduction to the phenomenon of surface tension as it holds together a large "bubble" of water on a penny. We pair the second activity with this to get more direct evidence of the effect of scale on structure. It dramatically shows that since volume-dependent weight increases faster than length-dependent surface tension, smaller "water domes" are rounder.

Floating Pins and Paper Clips

This is another activity giving direct experience with the effect of scale on structure. Large pins and paper clips sink to the bottom. Smaller ones "float." This is another scale effect.

The following activity provides an exciting culmination for the unit on scale and structure. Students can use all that they have learned to build something much bigger and better than they could have done before, thoughtfully predicting which structural elements and types of joints will give more strength and stability.

Garden Poles and Skewers—Building Up

Building up with these materials takes the students back to the kind of towers they were building at the beginning of the unit. We introduce this activity by showing students the garden poles and telling them that they will be building huge towers outdoors. Before they do so, they will build scale models of their design on their tabletop with bamboo skewers. Most groups build fine skewer towers indoors, but when they try to replicate their designs with the large-scale bamboo garden poles, things don't work the same. We suggest that students modify their design but keep a record of the changes they need to make. They eventually make towers that stand. These problem-solving opportunities can lead to lively discussions on scale effects.

The following activity is a repeat of an early unit activity. It allows for direct comparisons of student work at the beginning and end of the unit. See Assessment below for sample indicators of success.

Building Up—Assessment

As part of the assessment of student learning we have students return to the first *Straws and Pins—Building Up* tower-building activity. Their work on these towers helps us and the students see how much they have learned over the course of the unit.

After the unit we want to get students started on thinking about how the ideas encountered here might be applied in a broader way. The following video and discussion can help to do this.

Powers of Ten *Video and Discussion of Scale*

We round out our unit by showing the class the *Powers of Ten* video (see Appendix B), using it to initiate a discussion of scale in the world. This is done in an attempt to initiate broader generalizations from the experience of this unit. We introduce some of the examples from the *Beyond This Book* section here.

Classroom Management

Group Work

Most of the activities assume a familiarity and competence with working cooperatively in groups on the part of both student and teacher.

Although each activity has recommendations for group sizes, feel free to adjust and adapt for your particular situation. There are many sources and programs[1] to help students become comfortable with and competent in working together in groups.

Gender Issues

Watch out for the following trends:

◆ Boys tend to dominate general building areas to the exclusion of girls.

◆ In mixed-sex groups, sometimes boys will do all the building, and girls will be recorders or observers.

◆ Often boys will share information by "doing for" rather than by giving advice or ideas.

It is important to be aware of and to address these problems, should they arise. Some suggestions:

◆ Address problems in group discussion, perhaps coupled with role playing and writing.

◆ Establish a Girls' Day in the block area, or a free-time sign-up sheet for this area.

◆ Create single-sex groups for some activities.

◆ Assign specific group roles.

Age-Appropriate Activities

Keep in mind the students' developmental level and social maturity when choosing activities. You may need to modify activities to meet student needs.

Setting Limitations, Parameters, and Challenge Goals

◆ Before starting an activity, discuss expectations with the students.

◆ Include students in the setting of limits for challenge activities. For example, when working with *Straws and Pins—Building Up,* students start with undirected building and then move to more focused building. You could focus them by having them build towers that can hold weight. The children can use their experience to help set the challenge. Consider as a group such questions as, What should be the tower height? and/or What weight should the tower hold?

◆ Other questions may come up during the discussion or early in the building that can be decided as a group. For instance, Can you fasten the tower legs to the tabletop? Do you have to use all of the straws or all of the pins?

◆ When the time comes to test the towers, questions may come up about what is a fair test. For instance, Where is it fair to hang weights? Can you reposition weights as you go along?

The question of fair testing comes up often in this work. It is an important step in your students developing an idea of controlling variables and making comparisons to a standard.

Questioning Strategies*

Questioning is one of the most important tools in guiding and extending student learning. The examples listed here can help you develop your own strategies to enhance your students' work and thinking as they experience the scale and structure unit.

Attention-Focusing Questions

◆ Have you seen?

◆ Do you notice?

◆ What does it do?

◆ What do you see, feel, hear?

These questions help students focus on observation/details as well as connect them to the phenomena.

Measuring and Counting Questions

◆ How many?

◆ How long?

◆ How often?

---

*Adapted from Joe Elstgeest, "The Right Question at the Right Time," in *Primary Science: Taking the Plunge,* ed. Wynne Harlen (London: Heinemann Educational Books, 1985).

These questions help students develop confidence because they can be answered directly from the activity experience.

Comparison Questions

◆ In what ways are _____ the same/different?

◆ Can you describe an order or pattern to _____?

◆ In what ways can you classify/categorize _____?

These questions may be embedded in activities such as classifying, attribute games, and data tables. They can help students to focus their observations as well as to classify/categorize/order the materials or their findings.

Action Questions

◆ What happens if _____?

◆ What happens if you don't _____?

These questions help students explore new materials, properties, forces, and/or events. They can be answered by simple experimentation.

Problem-Posing Questions

◆ Can you find a way to _____?

These question involve students in authentic problem-solving situations. They support inquiry, critical thinking, and experimentation.

Reasoning Questions

◆ What do you think about _____?

◆ Why do you think that _____?

These questions stimulate students' reasoning and help them to draw conclusions and generalizations and to expand or change their ideas. Do not ask these questions until the students have had the experience they need to reason from evidence.

The questions above focus on guiding the children's investigation into the materials and concepts in the activities. It is also important to help them to look at their process of working through the activity and at their own thinking. The following questions have this goal, and are especially useful as writing prompts.*

Metacognitive Questions

◆ What have you discovered?

◆ How do you know?

◆ What do you wonder?

---

*Adapted from Jeanne Reardon, "Developing a Community of Scientists," in *Science Workshop,* ed. Wendy Saul et al. (Portsmouth, NH: Heinemann Educational Books, 1985).

- What will you do next? How do you decide what to do next?
- How do you decide what to record?
- What helps you do science?
- How do you know when to stop, that you are finished?
- Do you ever give up (abandon) your idea/question/ explanation? When? Why?
- What makes you reverse your explanation?

Assessment

Assessment is a tool for getting feedback about our teaching strategies. It guides us in making modifications or changes to our teaching, thereby strengthening our teaching and classroom curriculum design. We are constantly informally assessing our students' understanding and our own work in the classroom. Below are some assessment strategies that will assist you in the implementation of the activities in this book.

Before the Unit

Assessment starts before and at the very beginning of the unit. We want to know what knowledge, skills, and experience students bring to the unit.

Students' prior knowledge and experience serve as starting points for the unit and present possible connecting points between classroom experience and students' experience outside the classroom. It will help in determining which activities you choose, how you present them, and what level of challenge to set for students. This information also serves as a baseline from which to measure student growth.

Discussion and writing are two good means of ascertaining some of this early information. Many teachers start the unit with a discussion of structure and scale. Questions for structure discussion include:

- What is a structure? Give some examples.
- What are some structures in the natural world?
- What are some structures made by people?
- What are some things you already know about structures?
- What do you want to know about structures?

Questions for scale discussion include:

- What is scale?
- What are the differences between big and little things?
- Do you think giants are really possible? How about miniature people?
- What are some things you already know about scale?

Some of these same prompts work for writing. Another could be, Write about something that you have built. This could range from a dollhouse to a pillow fort.

Write about how you built it, what it looked like, what was the hardest part about building it, and what you used it for.

During the Unit

When we design a unit, we ask ourselves:

- What are the goals for the unit?

- What do we want the students to be learning?

- What activities will best help meet these goals?

- What will captivate student interest?

- What is the most effective mix and order of modes for presenting activities? (Here we look at grouping, pacing, order of activities, and mix of goal-oriented versus open-ended activities.)

As the unit progresses, we look to assessment to see if we are meeting the goals that we set and to give us clues to help modify or change instruction, grouping, pacing, or choice of the activities. After each activity we ask ourselves questions such as:

- Was the activity engaging for students? Were they focused?

- In what ways did the outcome match the objective? Do we need any modifications or adjustments in response to student interest or level of understanding?

The goals for the unit all involve student learning and construction of larger understanding. How do we know students are learning the basic ideas? How do we know an activity is helping us to meet our goals? We have found three areas particularly fruitful in looking for indicators of student learning. They involve 1) student action, 2) student speech, and 3) student writing and drawing.

1. Student Action

Observing student performance gives us information on the success of the activity in engaging student interest, and on the growth in student learning. If we are successful, then over the course of the unit we expect to see an increasing level of confidence, skill, and sophistication in students' approach to activities and in what they produce. For example, in the sample unit found in the previous section, students start out with a straws-and-pins structure. In their early building attempts we expect to see a lot of tentative starts, a number of structures that are unstable or don't stand at all, and many expressions of frustration. By the time they repeat this activity at the end of the unit, a sign of success would be their building with much less hesitation. They might proceed to build something quite substantial with few "fumbles," or they might try building something considerably more challenging and imaginative. There should be evidence both in the approach and in the final product that the student has applied newly gained understandings about structures.

2. Student Speech

Students' oral responses, questions, and observations made as part of whole-group or small-group discussion before, during, and after activities also give us information on student learning. One of the most straightforward things to do is to ask students what they have learned after an activity or set of activities. This not only gives you information but also prompts students' self-assessment. As the successful unit progresses, student oral responses become more specific. Their observations are more detailed and their questions become more sophisticated. For example, in the *Straws and Pins—Building Up* activity you may hear early comments like, "This is too hard," "I can't do it," or an all-too-early "I'm done." After more experience, comments can progress to, "I finally made it work by putting in some extra straws at the bottom."

3. Student Writing and Drawing

Students' written responses and drawings are another rich source of information. Many teachers use science logs or recording sheets to elicit writing. Students are usually given a question to respond to in writing or specifics to write about (see sample record sheets in Appendix D). In a successful unit, written responses will show some of the same types of changes as the oral responses. For example, in the *Straws and Pins—Building Up* activity, an early journal entry might read, "Today we built a tower. It was tall. I had fun." A later entry could be, "Today we built a tower that was two feet tall. We made the base wide so it wouldn't tip over. We used braces to make it stronger. We wonder if our tower will stand if we take some straws out."

At the beginning of the unit, students will draw or sketch their structures primarily as a way of "preserving" them. Students should be encouraged, throughout the unit, to use drawing as a tool for representing specific techniques or understandings that help them solve particular design problems. If they get this encouragement, then toward the end of the unit the students will show a greater range of drawings, illustrating progressively more sophisticated understandings.

End of the Unit

At the end of the unit, we look to assessment to inform us about how to teach this unit better in the future. We want to use all of the information we gathered during the unit to make this evaluation. In addition, assessment of overall student learning is useful in evaluating the unit. Many of the same areas mentioned above are useful here. You may want to choose a final activity to serve as a performance assessment. Discussion and writing about what they have learned allows students themselves to identify and articulate what it is they have learned. Discussion and writing that connects students' classroom learning to the world outside the classroom is especially helpful to check how your unit has affected student thinking about their world.

Notes

1. The following can help students learn to work in groups:

Jeanne Gibbs, *TRIBES: A Process for Social Development and Cooperative Learning* (Santa Rosa, Calif.: Center Source Publications, 1987).

David W. Johnson, Roger T. Johnson, and Edythe Johnson Holukes, *Cooperation in the Classroom,* 6th ed. (Minn.: Interaction Book Company, 1993).

PART ONE

The Physics and Engineering of Structure

> ## Note to the Teacher
>
> The following conceptual overview is for you. Its purpose is to provide you with a conceptual framework for organizing your teaching and responding to student discoveries. For your students, developing an understanding of these ideas will grow out of experiencing the phenomena which are inherent in the activities.
>
> You should not feel that you have to understand all of this information before you start teaching. Try these activities along with your students, using this conceptual overview as your own reference. Engaging in the activities will clarify many of the concepts for you as well as for your students.

Context

In this section, students will build a variety of structures using a variety of materials. The purpose of these activities is to give the students a feel for the materials and to show how the materials themselves dictate the nature of how they can be put together for stable structures. This section also introduces students to a number of the fundamental physical phenomena at play in the construction of buildings.

Concepts

When you build, you encounter a number of fundamental physical phenomena. In this section, we look at the building phenomena of forces, torque, center-of-mass, stability, tension and compression, and beam and column strength.

Forces

The primary force that affects your structure is the vertical force of gravity. The pull of gravity creates a downward force on the structure. This downward force consists of the weight of the structure itself (called the *dead load*), plus the weight of whatever sits, hangs, or walks on your structure (called the *live load*).

Different parts of the structure must support different weights. When you build a structure, think of it as being divided into layers. The top layer has no weight to support. The second layer must support the weight of the top layer. The third layer must support the weight of both the top and second layers. As you move down the structure, each "layer" must support a bit more weight than the one above it. Therefore, the lower layers must be stronger than the upper layers. The ground must support the weight of the entire structure, hence the need for a strong foundation.

Suppose you successfully build a 10-foot tower out of bamboo poles (as you may do in the *Garden Poles—Building Up* activity). The tower stands because each layer is strong enough to support all of the layers above it. Now suppose you want to place a 2-pound bag of sand on top of the tower. Your tower will have to support the additional 2 pounds of weight or it will break. It is an interplay of upward and downward forces which will decide your tower's fate.

These forces work together like this: The weight of the sandbag is a downward force on your tower. In order for the structure to stand, there must be an equal force pushing up on the sandbag. According to Newton's Laws, in order for objects at rest to stay at rest, the forces acting on them must balance out. When you build a structure, the strength of the materials you use as a frame and the other materials that bind them together provide an upward force to counteract the downward force of the weight. The forces that these structural materials exert are elastic or springlike in nature and act in response to an external force. When you put a weight on top of your tower, the vertical poles become slightly compressed. Like a spring, they push back. The activities in this section explore the different natures of varying materials.

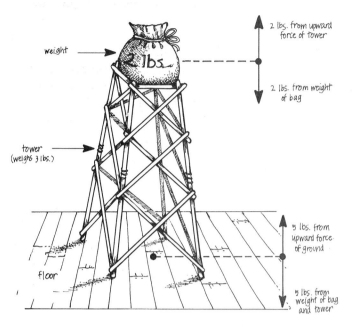

Think of these forces as a kind of reverse tug-of-war (instead of moving apart, they are moving toward each other). When you place the 2-pound sandbag on the tower top, there is a weight of 2 pounds being pulled toward the ground. If your structure is strong enough, it will exert an opposing force that *pushes up* at the sandbag with the equal force of 2 pounds. The two opposing forces pulling down (gravity) and pushing up (strength of structure) balance themselves at zero, and there is no movement. By analogy, in a tug-of-war, the red flag would remain stationary over the middle line. This state is called *equilibrium*. If the tower is not strong enough to exert 2 pounds of force upward, gravity will prevail and the sandbag will come crashing to the ground, pulling the tower with it. In a game of tug-of-war, one side would have lost.

The floor on which the tower sits must also be strong enough to support the weight of both the tower and the sandbag. If the tower itself weighs 3 pounds and a 2-pound sandbag is added to it, then there is a downward force of 5 pounds on the floor. The tower must be able to push up with 2 pounds of force against the sandbag, while the floor must be strong enough to push up with a force of 5 pounds against the combination of the sandbag and the tower. The floor acts as a foundation, supporting the entire load.

In addition to weight, there are other kinds of loads or forces that can act on structures, including wind, earthquakes, and those caused by temperature changes. For all of these forces, the structure must be strong enough to exert a counterbalancing force in order to maintain a state of equilibrium and not collapse.

Torque

There are other considerations besides the balance of forces which you must take into account when building your tower. You might think that if your tower is able to exert an upward force of two pounds when you place a 2-pound bag of sand on its top layer, then it will maintain equilibrium and continue to stand. But this is not necessarily so! You must also consider the distribution of weight. If the top of your 10-foot bamboo tower has a horizontal flagpole, and you hang the 2-pound sandbag on the end of this flagpole, the same tower may collapse, because the weight of the sandbag, extended out from the tower, creates a *torque* on the tower. If the tower cannot exert a counteracting torque, the tower will pivot about its feet and fall over, the victim of an unbalanced torque.

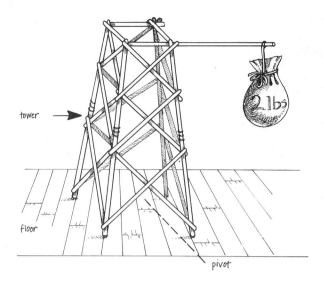

tower

floor

pivot

Try this: Hold your arm straight out. Hang a heavy purse or bag on your arm, near your shoulder. Now move it out toward your wrist. It feels heavier on your wrist than it did on your shoulder, even though the weight of the purse has not changed. It's the combination of the weight of the bag (a downward force) and the *distance* between the bag and your shoulder (the pivot point) that creates the effect which tires your arm. That's torque: the combination of force and distance from a pivot point (torque = force × distance).

In the case of the 10-foot bamboo tower, the torque is equal to the force from the weight of the sandbag times the distance the sandbag is extended out from the tower. The pivot point is a line where the tower meets the ground on the side where the sandbag is hanging. The effects of torque are twisting and rotation.

Imagine this: Balance a 6-foot board on a pivot which allows the board to seesaw up and down. Put a 2-pound block on each end of the board. The board doesn't collapse because it is strong enough to push up with 4 pounds of force, maintaining equilibrium. The board is balanced, and does not seesaw or rotate, because the torque on the right (the weight of the block times the distance from the pivot point) is balanced by the torque on the left. (On each side, the torque is equal to 2 pounds × 3 feet, weight × distance from the pivot point.) This state is called *rotational equilibrium*.

Now, upset the balance of torques: Move the block on the right halfway between the end and the pivot point. Since the distance has decreased for the right block, so has its torque. (Left torque equals 2 pounds × 3 feet = 6 foot-pounds; right

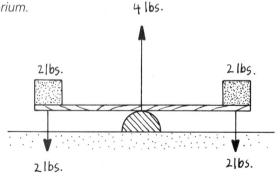

torque equals 2 pounds × 1.5 feet = 3 foot-pounds) The board will rotate down toward the left, where the torque is greater. If you now add another 2-pound block to the right side, for a total of 4 pounds, but place both blocks at the midpoint, the torques will be balanced and the board will not rotate (left torque equals 2 pounds × 3 feet = 6 foot-pounds; right torque equals 4 pounds × 1.5 feet = 6 foot-pounds).

It's not only the weight . . . it's where you put the weight that counts.

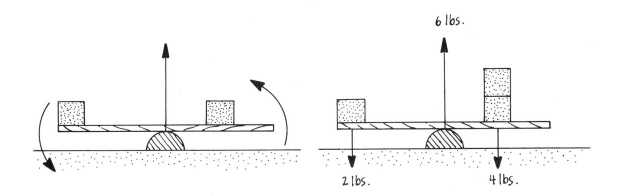

Center-of-Mass

The center-of-mass is the point of balance for any object. Understanding the location of the center-of-mass is a key to maintaining a balance of torques and keeping a structure standing. In people, the center-of-mass (when we are standing or lying straight) is around our belly buttons. If you ever have to lie down on your stomach and reach over a cliff to pull something up, you don't want to lean out so far that your belly button is looking down over the side of the cliff. Chances are your balance would be upset (and so would your temperament) as you tumbled into the abyss.

The center-of-mass isn't always a physical point (or a button); it can be a location in the middle of a group of objects. Try this: Set the 6-foot board on the pivot again. Put two 2-pound blocks in the middle of each side of the board. The torque on each side is equal to 4 pounds × 1.5 feet = 6 foot-pounds. Now, on the right side, put your hands on both of the blocks and slide them by equal amounts in opposite directions. (Slide one block 6 inches toward the pivot points, and the other 6 inches toward the end.) The board will remain balanced—retaining its rotational equilibrium—because the center-of-mass of the two blocks on the right remains at 1.5 feet from the pivot, which is exactly where the center-of-mass is for the two blocks on the left.

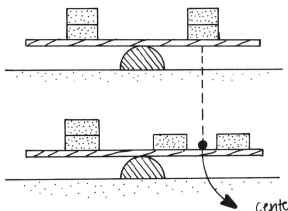

center of mass of two weights

One more example: Place a 4-foot bamboo pole over the side of a table, so that three feet of it is hanging in midair. Anchor the other end of the pole to the table. Now make a bundle of four sticks and tie it tightly to the end which is in midair. The weight of these four sticks will cause the bamboo pole to bend slightly. Now undo the bundle and arrange the sticks so that they are joined by their ends into one long stick. Attach one of the ends of this long

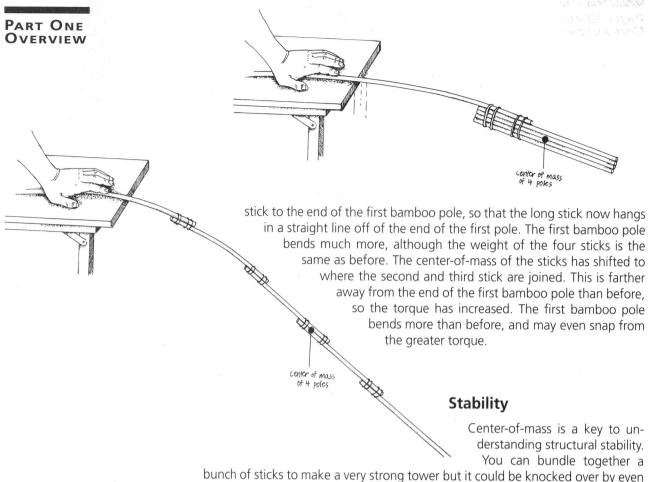

center of mass
of 4 poles

stick to the end of the first bamboo pole, so that the long stick now hangs in a straight line off of the end of the first pole. The first bamboo pole bends much more, although the weight of the four sticks is the same as before. The center-of-mass of the sticks has shifted to where the second and third stick are joined. This is farther away from the end of the first bamboo pole than before, so the torque has increased. The first bamboo pole bends more than before, and may even snap from the greater torque.

center of mass
of 4 poles

Stability

Center-of-mass is a key to understanding structural stability. You can bundle together a bunch of sticks to make a very strong tower but it could be knocked over by even the slightest breeze. The bundled sticks lack stability. Intuitively, you know that if you make a broad base for the sticks, the tower will stand—why is that?

Imagine a line that falls from the center-of-mass of the bundle of sticks to the ground. The force of gravity pulling at the structure travels along this line, and the strength of the structure pushes up through it. This balance of forces keeps the structure erect, as we saw in the *Forces* section above. A structure becomes unbalanced when it is tilted so that the center-of-mass is shifted outside the base of the object—the imaginary line which connects the center-of-mass to the ground does not go through the bundle, but outside of the bundle. Without the support of the sticks to counteract the force of gravity, the bundle falls. To ensure stability, the center-of-mass must lie directly over the base of an object.

bundle of sticks

wood base

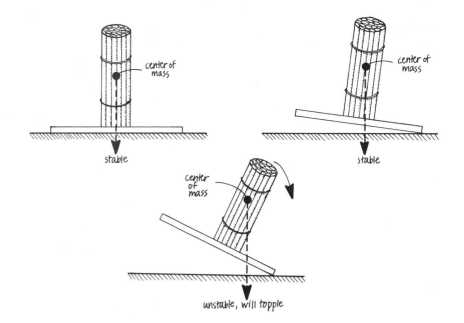

In sports, dance, and loading trucks, we are told that a low center-of-mass gives us more stability. This can be understood as follows: with a high center-of-mass, it only takes a small lean one way or another to make the center-of-mass go outside the base. An object with a lower center-of-mass, leaning at the same angle, can keep its center-of-mass over the base and remain standing.

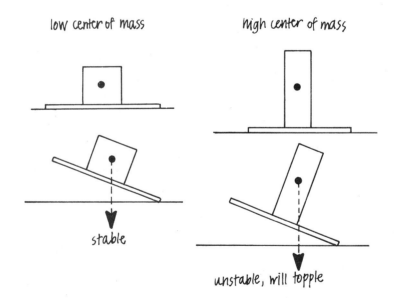

Channeling Loads

The purpose of structure is to channel loads on the building to the ground. The action is similar to that of water flowing down a network of pipes; columns, beams, cables, arches, and other structural elements act as pipes for the flow of the loads. . . . The remarkable inherent simplicity of nature allows the structure to perform its task through two elementary actions only: pulling and pushing. Many and varied as the loads may be and geometrically complicated as the structure may be, its elements never develop any other kind of action. They are either pulled by loads, and then they stretch, or they are pushed, and then they shorten. In structural language, the loads are said to stress the structure, which strains under the stress.
— Mario Salvadori, *Why Buildings Stand Up*

Tension and Compression

When a material is pulled apart, it is said to be in *tension*. Tension lengthens materials. If we pull on both ends of a rubber band, it becomes longer. When a material is pushed together, it is said to be under *compression*. Compression is the opposite of tension: it shortens materials. If we push on the top and bottom of a sponge,

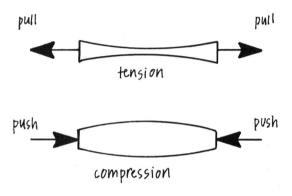

the sponge becomes shorter. The forces which act on structural elements are all pushes or pulls tending to pull pieces apart or push pieces together. Through pushing and pulling (tension and compression), a building must retain its stability.

Since all structural action consists of tension and/or compression, all structural materials must be strong in one or both. Steel cable is very strong in tension but has no strength in compression. Concrete is very strong in compression but much weaker in tension. Materials like wood and aluminum are strong in both tension and compression. Look around the room and out the window and find examples of tension and compression. Crossbars in buildings are used to keep components from flying apart; a crossbar is being pulled in both directions, therefore it is under tension. Doorjambs are being pushed by the weight of the floor and ceiling; they are therefore under compression.

Try this: make a triangular section by pinning three drinking straws together into a triangle. Place one of the straws on the table to act as the base of the triangle. Now push down on the top of the triangle where the two upper straws are joined. When you push down on the straws, the table is pushing back up; the side straws experience compression, and are infinitesimally shortened. But the two straws are also being forced apart at the base of the triangle. If you remove the pin where one of the straws is joined to the base, you can see that the straw will move away from the base straw. The bottom straw of the triangle has been experiencing tension, holding the two other straws together.

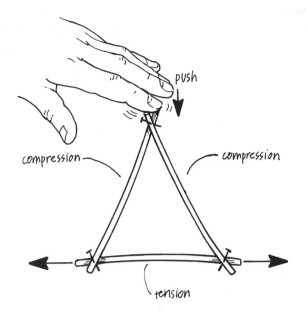

Triangular sections are very common in buildings due to their inherent rigidity. Try this: make a triangular section by pinning three drinking straws together into a triangle and a square section by pinning four straws together to make a square. Notice how the square section collapses as you push or pull on it, whereas the triangular section remains rigid. The square section can be made more stable by pinning in a diagonal brace, thus creating a triangle.

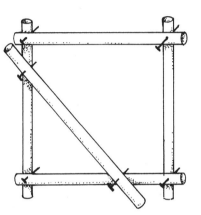

Beam and Column Strength

When individual sticks bend, they experience both tension and compression. Try this: slowly bend a stick in your hands until it breaks. Notice how the fibers on the outside of the curve are pulled apart, and those on the inside are squeezed together. The outer part of the curve is experiencing tension, while the inner is experiencing compression.

This is exactly what happens when a load is placed on a beam that is fastened or held up on both ends. The top side of the beam experiences a very small amount of compression from the weight of the load, while the bottom side experiences the comparable tension. However, the middle axis of the beam is not stressed at all. This unstressed middle (neutral) axis through the beam is called the *horizontal plane.* When you place a load on a beam, most of the force of compression or tension falls at the farthest points from the middle axis. This is why tubes are so strong; most of their material lies on the edges of the tube, precisely where most of the forces are exerted. You will see this illustrated in the bridge-building activities.

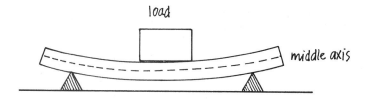

beam supported at both ends

The beams described above were supported from both ends. Beams supported at one end, as in the building out or cantilever activities, behave in a similar manner. There is still an unstressed middle axis. However, in these cases the compression from the weight of the load is on the bottom of the beam, and the top of the beam experiences tension.

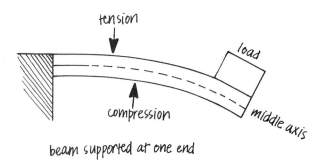

beam supported at one end

Columns exhibit similar effects. Rather than simply compressing and crumbling under a load, most columns bend and buckle. As the column bends, one side is stretched, experiencing tension, and the opposite side shrinks, experiencing compression. The unstressed middle axis through the column is called the *central vertical axis*. We see illustrations of this in the *Clay Towers* activity and many other tower-building activities.

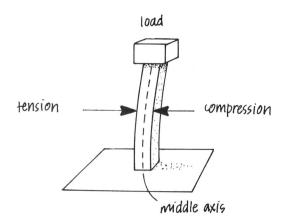

BUILDING UP

The activities in this subsection provide a good starting point for your students to experience building. They will become familiar with working with materials while they experience many of the basic physics and engineering concepts inherent in structures. Building up and making tall structures emphasize the concepts of balancing the forces of weight with the strength of materials as well as stability and tension and compression.

Building-up activities provide a good opportunity for your students to talk and/or write about the tall structures that they know. Skyscrapers are obvious, but what about tall trees, giraffes, construction cranes, broadcast towers, or antennae? Telephone poles, basketball poles, and chalkboards provide close-at-hand opportunities for observation. Early discussion of examples like these invite your students to bring their outside experience into their explorations. You can make the connection to students' out-of-school experience even stronger if, during the unit, you and your class go on an outing to look at examples of tall structures.

General Building

Time

◆ 20–40 minutes

Preparation

◆ Clear away a large working space, either on tables or the floor.

Grouping

◆ Groups of two to six depending on age, temperament, and resources; students will sometimes work alone or together.
◆ This also works well as a self-directed center.

Materials

◆ Small wooden unit blocks
◆ Optional: Any standard student building material, such as Lincoln Logs™, dominoes, Cuisenaire rods™, Legos™, playing cards, etc.

Teacher Tips

◆ Ask students to bring blocks from home. Have them label their blocks so that they don't get misplaced or mixed up with the others.

Context

When students build with blocks (or any building material) they are generally seeking just a few things: aesthetic achievement, stability, and—quite often—magnitude. Building with blocks, in the context of other structure and scale activities, can help students see the link between structure, scale, and stability. It provides experience with the physics and engineering of structures. It also allows them to explore the building potentials and limitations of the materials.

This activity provides a good general background to all aspects of structure and scale, or it can be used to reinforce the lessons of more focused building activities. Building of any sort provides experiences that will prove to be of great value when the students plunge into a more organized structure and scale unit. The more of this they can get, the better.

What It Is

Ask the students to take the blocks and work together to "build something." This kind of open-ended investigation allows the students to interact with the materials on their own terms. The teacher serves to guide and stretch student thinking by incorporating structure and scale vocabulary and asking questions. Teachers can also suggest interesting extensions, e.g., building on an incline, building out from the edge of a tabletop.

Discussing Results

Have the students share their structures with each other. What difficulties did they encounter and how did they solve them? Have them describe their structure and, perhaps, give it a name. Try to have them talk about how balance, stability, and downward pull (gravity) affected their building.

Possible questions to ask:

◆ Did anything surprise you?

◆ Did you have a plan before you began to build or did it evolve?

◆ Is there a way you could make your building stronger? bigger?

◆ When did your building collapse? Why did it collapse? What did you do to fix the problem?

◆ What would happen if your structure was pushed in a certain area? pulled?

◆ Does your structure look like something you have seen somewhere else?

General Building

What's Going On

All building activities give a broad range of contexts in which to encounter structural concepts. This one, in that it is free-form, allows the students to experience, discover, and develop an intuition for some of the basic physics concepts covered in *The Physics and Engineering of Structure*.

Extensions

◆ You can do the same type of general building activity with many different building materials. Each material will have its own potential and limitations. For example, you could use Lincoln Logs™, dominoes, Cuisenaire™ rods, or Legos™. You could even use sugar cubes left over from the *Growing Cubes* activity.

◆ You could also have the students place or hang weights on their structures to test the strength and stability of various structural elements.

◆ Since students may want to keep a record of their structures, this activity provides a good opportunity to have them draw a picture and write a story about their work in their journals.

◆ For connections to their outside experience, you might have the students collect drawings or photos of neighborhood structures. Have the students compare and contrast their structures to the ones in the photos.

Straws and Pins—Building Up

TIME

- 45 minutes for exploration
- At least 1 hour for challenge

PREPARATION

- Separate the materials into packets for each pair.

GROUPING

- Students may work individually or together in pairs. If students have not had much experience building with a partner, this can pose a challenge. You may want to model appropriate behavior (see *Teaching Scale and Structure*).

MATERIALS

(per pair)

- 50 plastic straws
- 50 straight pins or paper clips
- Scissors, for cutting straws
- 10 weights (e.g., large washers or film canisters filled with sand)
- Yardstick or meterstick (can be shared by groups)

TEACHER TIPS

- Use pins only if you think it's safe. Talk about pin safety and rules for working with pins. Rules might include no traveling with the pins, or that pins must stay on the tables or in the straws. Warn students about pricking their fingers.
- Have students take the paper off straws the day before—they'll then be curious about the upcoming activity.

Context

Building up with straws and pins provides students the opportunity to experience many of the basic physics and engineering concepts inherent in structures. Tall structures emphasize concepts such as balancing the forces of weight and the strength of materials as well as stability, tension, and compression.

Ask students about the tall structures that they know. Not only skyscrapers and monuments but basketball poles and trees will come to mind. Discussion of their out-of-school familiarity with built-up structures will help them to connect what they learn in this activity with what they know outside the classroom.

You can do the activity early in a unit, and then try variations at a later time.

What It Is

As with any new material, it is important to give your students time to freely explore with the straws and pins. (Some teachers prefer to use straws and paper clips to avoid problems of getting stuck by pins, especially with younger students.) To push students in the direction of building up, ask your students to use 50 straws and 50 pins to build something taller than it is wide. Allow the students to explore their ideas. As their structures begin to take shape, suggest that they use bent paper clips as hangers for weights to test the physical strength of the structures.

After the free exploration, perhaps at the second session, pose one or more of the following challenges using 50 straws and 50 pins:

◆ What is the highest structure you can build?

◆ Can you build a 3-foot tower that will hold three sand-filled canisters?

◆ Build the strongest 2-foot tower that you can.

◆ What is the highest structure that you can build that will hold one sand-filled canister?

◆ What are the fewest straws that you can use to build a 3-foot tower?

The question of rules and what is fair inevitably arises in these challenges. This is an important question as it forms the basis for scientific objectivity. You and the class must define your parameters: Is it fair to anchor the tower legs to the table or floor? Can your tower lean against the wall? Where is it fair to hang the weights? For instance, for the sake of fair comparisons, you and your students may decide that to test the strong 2-foot tower all weights must hang from a single bent paper clip hooked onto a point which is at least 2 feet high. In setting this condition, students are recognizing that both weight and position (where you hang the weight) are variables in this experiment. In order to get "fair" results, you must change only one variable (the weight) and keep the other variable (where you hang it) unchanged.

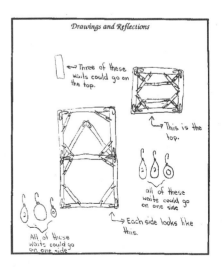

Go to middle for Clay Bridges

Straw Towers

Observations:
- Connecting the straws and paper clips worked really well.
- cross-bracing made the straw towers very strong.
- it had to be supportive on the bottom.
- don't put too many waits on one side.
- put waits all around the straw towers.

Questions:
- How many waits can I put on one side?
- What would happen if the straws were longer?
- What would happen if I put the waits on the bottom part of the tower?
- What would it be like if we had something different to connect the straws?

Drawings and Reflections

Three of these waits could go on the top.

This is the top.

all of these waits could go on one side

Each side looks like this.

All of these waits could go on one side

Throughout the building process, the students should be encouraged to test the strength, stability, and durability of the structures they are working on. At the end of the building process, students should have the opportunity to observe and discuss each other's structures. For challenges involving strength, test each structure one by one, so that the students as a class can learn from the efforts of their peers.

Discussing Results

Have the students share their results of free exploration with the whole class. Record their discoveries on the chalkboard or chart paper. Some towers may not be successful. This presents an opportunity to discuss how you often learn more by experimenting with something new, even when it doesn't work, than from something that is true but tried. Underscore the importance of this for learning science.

In the challenge activities, issues of winners and losers may arise. Look for various criteria to judge buildings, including the degree of risk, dimension, and stability. The smallest structure may be the most stable, the most innovative may have collapsed early on. Emphasize what lessons were learned from each structure.

During testing with weights, raising questions like the following can help the students see some of the implications of what they are doing:

◆ How many weights can be hung before the structure collapses?

◆ Does it matter where the weights are hung?

◆ Will the structure be more likely to collapse if the weights are hung in one place or spread out?

◆ Predict where the structure will weaken first. How might that area be strengthened so that another area will collapse first?

In discussing any structure, special attention should be paid to structural elements that worked well, or that the students learned to avoid. Students should be asked what made it work or not work well. For example, triangular sections and diagonal bracing are essential in straw-and-pin structures.

Questions about which straws are being pulled (i.e., can be replaced by strings) and which are being pushed help bring out the concepts of tension and compression (see the overview of *The Physics and Engineering of Structure* for more details).

What's Going On

When constructing with straws and pins, many physics and engineering concepts come into play to ensure or defeat stability. Your class can directly observe

◆ tension and compression

◆ the use of triangular versus square elements and the need for diagonal bracing

◆ the introduction of broad bases

◆ the effects of weight distribution

◆ balance.

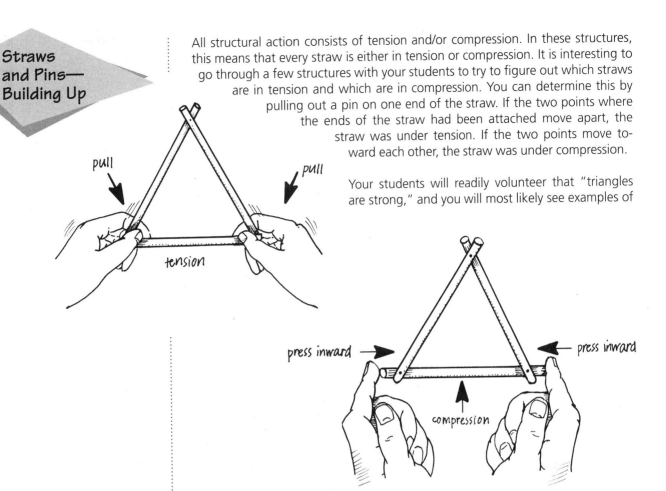

All structural action consists of tension and/or compression. In these structures, this means that every straw is either in tension or compression. It is interesting to go through a few structures with your students to try to figure out which straws are in tension and which are in compression. You can determine this by pulling out a pin on one end of the straw. If the two points where the ends of the straw had been attached move apart, the straw was under tension. If the two points move toward each other, the straw was under compression.

Your students will readily volunteer that "triangles are strong," and you will most likely see examples of

pull

pull

tension

press inward

press inward

compression

the use of diagonal bracing to stabilize square sections. You can also ask students where they have seen these shapes in real-world structures. You find them in bridges, broadcast towers, and pylons supporting high-voltage electrical wires. Diagonal bracing can be seen in the structures supporting wooden decks. This engineering principle is quite evident when you work with these materials.

Many of your students' towers will collapse by toppling over to one side. They will find that broader bases give them more stability. Also, hanging weights high on a tower is more likely to topple the tower then hanging weights down low. When the balance point of a tower (its center-of-mass) is not directly over the base, the tower topples over. Your students will get lots of experience with this. (See the discussion of center-of-mass and stability in the overview of *The Physics and Engineering of Structure* for more on this subject.)

Pin joints are common in real structures. For instance, rivets are used with steel beams and nails are used with wood planks in the same way that pins are used with straws in this activity.

Extensions

◆ Students should be encouraged to test the strength, stability, and durability of their structures. In this way, they gain insight into the behavior of structures that are subjected to outside forces, and they can see how to improve their structures so as to strengthen weak points. In addition to hanging weights on structures, they can be "wind tested" using a large piece of cardboard as a fan or by taking them outside into a real wind. You can also leave the structures intact overnight, to discover which ones are still standing in the morning.

◆ Conduct a search for unnecessary straws. Ask the builders if they think there is a straw that could be cut which would not make the whole thing fall down. Have them try it. If it works, could they cut another straw? How many cuts do they think it will take before the structure collapses? Could they build a structure that could not stand many cuts?

◆ Have the students take a set of materials home to build a structure with their family. They can draw or photograph their structure and write about what they did.

Toothpicks and Clay

TIME

◆ 40–60 minutes

PREPARATION

◆ Set out materials.

GROUPING

◆ Individuals or pairs

MATERIALS
(per student or pair)

◆ 2 oz. plasticene (modeling clay)
◆ 50 round toothpicks

TEACHER TIPS

◆ Using a relatively stiff plasticene is very important. Some types are very soft, especially in a warm room. Working with soft clay can be extremely frustrating.
◆ Plasticene is an oil-based clay, and leaves an oily residue on surfaces. Work on paper and/or be prepared to clean with soap or other grease remover.
◆ Discuss "clay etiquette" with your students. Clay should stay on the work surface. No traveling with the toothpicks or clay.

Context

This activity helps students develop an understanding of three-dimensional structures. They can explore how their structures' stability, strength, and balance are directly affected by the structural/architectural designs they create. This relationship is emphasized by the difficulties encountered due to the weakness of the clay joints. This differs from activities like *Straws and Pins—Building Up,* where the weaker elements are the struts (straws) rather than the joints (pins). It gives students another way of looking at structure.

Many students bring the experience of working with plasticene to this activity. A preliminary discussion of how they think the material will behave helps to incorporate their previous experience.

What It Is

Have the students make clay balls to use as connectors with the toothpicks. Students will almost invariably start by making a "porcupine" (one ball of clay with all of the toothpicks sticking out). Give them some time to do such experimentation before they get down to more goal-oriented building. Ask them to use the two materials to make sculptures which

♦ are freestanding on a level surface

♦ can support their own weight

♦ are not anchored by another material to the table surface.

To begin, ask questions like:

♦ In what ways can you use the clay balls to connect the toothpicks?

♦ How can you make your sculpture stable?

♦ How will your sculpture be interesting?

♦ What happens when you build up/out?

Students can make the clay balls any size they choose. You might want to discuss beforehand the possible differences between large balls and small balls. You might also choose to limit the materials to even fewer than 50 toothpicks; if so, have the students participate in setting the limits.

Discussing Results

Ask the following questions:

♦ How did you begin building?

♦ Did the size of the clay connectors make a difference? Are they all about the same size throughout your structure?

Many students make increasingly smaller balls as the structure gets taller. This question focuses their attention on that fact.

♦ What did you do to make your structure more stable as it got taller?

Students often broaden the base to increase stability. Ask:

♦ Did any shapes seem stronger than others?

♦ What materials could have made your sculpture bigger or stronger?

♦ What kinds of things did you do to keep your structure from collapsing? What worked/didn't work?

What's Going On

As the structures grow, the clay connectors show their weakness because of the increased weight they must support. Students tend to make the clay balls on the top smaller to reduce weight. They sense that the bottom layer must support all of the weight of the top layers. Students can also see that as their structures get taller, the bases must get wider to preserve stability.

As the structure becomes taller, it begins to twist. It tends to collapse into itself like a coiling snake rather than collapsing by tipping over or folding in half. Engineers describe this in energy terms, saying that the structure seeks its least energy. For our purposes, it is best to talk about this in terms of the structure finding the easiest way to handle the forces on it or the easiest way to collapse.

Extensions

The large number of suggested extensions for this activity give breadth and range to possible student experience. It is valuable to consider doing a number of them.

◆ Do the same activity with different joiners. Try using gumdrops or miniature marshmallows which have been left out for a few days (and which have become slightly hardened). Discuss how the building was different with these stronger joiners.

◆ Do the same activity with different struts. Try using uncooked spaghetti instead of toothpicks. Discuss how the building was different with these materials.

◆ Build sculptures that have different numbers of clay ball "feet" (i.e., balls that touch the table) and compare the strength and stability of structures with 1, 2, 3, and 4 feet.

◆ Build structures with defined shapes—squares, cubes, triangles, pyramids, poly-hedrons, octagonal bases.

◆ After students have finished their sculptures, see what happens when you begin to remove the toothpicks. The idea is that some of the toothpicks may not be central to the structure's stability. Generally, this process works best if the students identify which toothpicks can be removed first. This process provides a particularly rich opportunity for discussion, as the results are often surprising.

◆ Have the students draw their structures and describe in writing the different approaches and structural aspects of each sculpture.

◆ Have the students draw side views (front and side) of the sculptures. Mix up the drawings and see if the students can identify whose sculpture is whose.

◆ Add small weights to the sculptures to observe structural integrity. Where do the structures bend, collapse, or topple?

◆ Ask the students to predict how high they could build with a given amount of materials.

◆ Have the students use a piece of yarn or string to measure the heights of their structures. Look at the tallest structures to see if there are similar features. Do the same for the smaller structures.

Clay Towers

TIME

◆ 20–40 minutes

PREPARATION

◆ Set out materials.

GROUPING

◆ Pairs or individuals

MATERIALS
(per pair or individual)

◆ 8 oz. plasticene (modeling clay)
◆ Yardsticks or metersticks

TEACHER TIPS

◆ Plasticene is an oil-based clay, and leaves an oily residue on surfaces. Work on paper and/or be prepared to clean with soap or other grease remover.

Context

Clay (plasticene) is a building material with which students usually have had some experience. They frequently attempt to make realistic figures with it, such as people, animals, or buildings. Clay is a good material for this activity since it is familiar and salvageable. The material allows the students to reconstruct after their first attempt collapses.

This activity fits well into transitions from general building to more focused investigations of the elements of structure and the effects of scale on those elements.

What It Is

In this activity, students are challenged to build a tall tower out of clay. You may want to begin by talking about towers and other tall things which will be familiar to the students: tetherball poles, electric pylons, the Empire State Building, or the Eiffel Tower. You might also want to ask the students questions like, "What kinds of things have you made before out of clay?" "What happened when you tried to build something tall?"

Ask the students to build the tallest freestanding tower that they can make with the half-pound of clay on their desks. Have other criteria for success besides that

Clay Towers

of tallness, so that the students whose buildings are short, or collapse, don't feel as if they've failed. Alternative criteria might include smoothness, lumpiness, style, originality, or humor.

Students will often begin by making the base so wide that they run out of clay before the tower is very tall, or they might make the base so narrow that the tower topples very quickly. They soon begin to understand the concept of graduating the thickness.

Some students will mold clumps of clay into towers, others will form bricks or balls and press them together. Through this process, they will come to understand the utility of joints that hold the separate "bricks" or "balls" together.

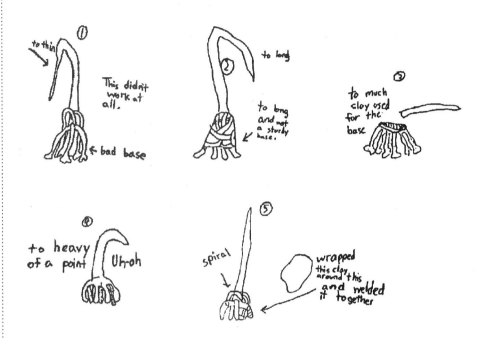

Discussing Results

Have the students discuss what was successful and what was difficult about the process.

Plot the tower heights on a graph, rounding to the nearest inch. This will be a bar graph showing how many towers were 4 inches tall, how many were 6 inches, how many 7 inches, etc. This graph helps convince students that there is a natural limit to the height of these towers independent of the skill of the builder.

The following questions might be useful:

◆ How did you begin building?

◆ What allowed you to go higher?

◆ Did you expect it to fall? Why?

◆ What made your tower collapse? Where was it weak and where was it strong?

◆ What would you do differently next time? Why?

43

◆ Did there seem to be a maximum height?

◆ What would you do to make an even taller structure?

◆ Is there another material which would allow you to make it taller?

◆ What questions do you have?

What's Going On

In general, the tallest towers will be symmetric, wide at the bottom, and tapered at the top. You can conceptualize tower building as adding thin layers from the top down. Each successive layer has to support the weight of all of the layers above it. Therefore, those at the top, which have little weight to bear, can be narrow and small, while those at the bottom must be broad and strong. Upper layers must balance over the lower ones since clay does not efficiently support shear forces. This is the type of force exerted by, for instance, pruning shears or scissors. It occurs when two parallel, opposite forces are not quite collinear (along the same line). This creates the need for symmetry.

The towers may also start to twist if they are top-heavy or if a column of clay is insufficiently supported. Tension and compression are easily visible in this material when the column collapses.

Extensions

◆ Have the students predict results if the amount of clay were doubled. One third grader commented in her picture-report that it would not be possible to make a tower with twice the clay twice as tall, because too much would have to be used to make the base "sterdy," thus limiting the height. Another predicted that with twice the clay he could construct a tower one-and-a-half times the height of his current tower. Ask the students to test their predictions with double the clay. This extension introduces the key idea that you cannot always keep the same shape (proportions) when you scale up.

◆ Have the students predict the results if more or less clay is used. Try half as much. Try one-tenth. Try six times as much. Ask the students to test their predictions with clay. They may have to combine their clay with that of others to test the larger predictions.

◆ Draw parallels to the natural world. For example, look at the tall shallow-rooted trees of the rain forest. How do these structures stand? What structural accommodations have they made? Why do they have to be so tall?

Garden Poles— Building Up

TIME

- Several 1–2 hour sessions
- Final session may take up to half a day.

PREPARATION

- Bundle poles and tape for each group.
- Reserve a large space, like part of a playground, for both building and storing between sessions.

GROUPING

- Four or five per group

MATERIALS
(per group)

- 35–60 4-foot bamboo garden stakes
- One roll of $\frac{3}{4}$-inch masking tape
- Matte knives or scissors
- Optional: a plastic bucket and 10 one-pound bags of sand

TEACHER TIPS

- You'll need a lot of space for construction and collapse.
- Taking photographs or videos helps to record student efforts and makes the deconstruction of their structures less dramatic.
- Use matte knives or scissors to take apart the structures.

Context

Building up with garden poles and tape provides students with the opportunity to experience the same basic physics and engineering phenomena they encountered in activities such as *Straws and Pins—Building Up* and *Toothpicks and Clay,* but on a large scale. The change in scale allows the students an entirely different experience of the phenomena. Materials seem more flimsy, joints seem less secure. This is a good activity to do near the end of your scale and structure unit, and should be preceded by building on a smaller scale. As in the smaller scale building-up activities, students should be given the opportunity to talk about tall structures that they know.

Building on this scale provides a perfect opportunity to discuss the students' different experiences doing building activities at different scales. For more discussion of this, see the *Skewers and Poles—Building Up* activity in the *Effect of Scale on Structure* section.

What It Is

For most students, working with these materials will feel very different from the other building that they have done. The students need an initial session where they can get familiar with the materials. In this session, ask the students to build a self-standing structure using 35 bamboo garden stakes and masking tape. Give them the following rules for building:

◆ The tape can only be wrapped twice around any given joint or stick.

◆ When joining sticks in a straight line, the sticks may only be taped together at two points (at each of these points, the piece of tape may only be wrapped around twice).

garden poles taped together in two spots

At the end of the session, record their accomplishments through video or photography, or by having the students draw pictures of their structures. Then have the students deconstruct the structures so that the poles can be used again at the next session.

At the next several sessions, using the same building rules as before, challenge the students to do one of the following:

◆ Build a structure that is taller than it is wide.

◆ Build a structure $6\frac{1}{2}$ feet tall that can hold the weight of a book.

◆ Using a maximum of 60 garden stakes, build a 12-foot-tall structure. This structure will probably have to be built on its side and then raised, or built in various stages: bottom, middle, top. You may want to modify the connecting rules for this. An additional challenge might be to ask, "Which group can do this using the fewest number of poles?" or "Which group can build the tallest tower?"

◆ Challenge the students to build a 12-foot structure (using 60 garden stakes) which can hold at least a 1-pound load. After they have completed their structures, stand on a ladder and hang a plastic bucket from the top of the structure, while the students watch at a safe distance from the base of the structures. Begin to add 1-pound bags of sand to the bucket one at a time. As the structure starts to respond to the load (by leaning, compressing, or swaying), have the students predict how many more bags the structure will hold and how the structure will break.

Choose the difficulty of the challenge based on the age and level of the building skills of your students. It is especially important in this activity to be sensitive to the issue of creating winners and losers. Student groups put a lot of time and effort into these structures and may feel bad if their tower doesn't measure up. Setting a challenge level which most students can meet and allowing them to go beyond this level is one strategy that has proven useful. Look for various criteria to judge buildings, including the degree of risk, stability, and innovation.

A particularly important criterion for these structures is aesthetics. Aesthetics is not just how pretty a structure is, but also how it makes the observer feel. Does the structure seem heavy? Is it open, light, and airy? Does it create a feeling of tension, as if something is about to happen any second? Does it create an image of movement? These garden pole structures may be considered sculptures and looked at in those terms.

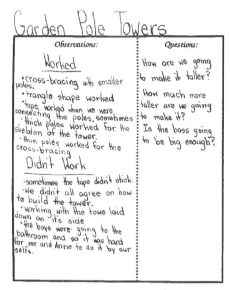

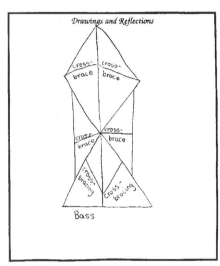

Discussing Results

After the initial session, have students share their results of free exploration with the whole class. Record their discoveries on the chalkboard or chart paper. Ask:

◆ What happened when they were building?

◆ What did they find out about building with these materials?

◆ What difficulties did they encounter and how did they resolve them?

◆ How would they build their towers differently if they were to do it again?

The final building session is followed by weight testing, measurement, and discussion. Ask:

◆ What physical phenomena did they observe?

◆ If their structure was wobbly, how did they stabilize it?

With structures that are tested with weights, raising questions like the following can help the students see some of the physical implications of what they are doing:

◆ How many weights can be hung before the structure collapses?

◆ Does it matter where the weights are hung?

◆ Will the structure be more likely to collapse if the weights are hung in one place or spread out?

◆ Predict where the structure will weaken first. Can that area be strengthened so that another area will collapse first?

Questions about which poles are being bent, and which poles are being pulled out of their taped joints, help emphasize the concepts of tension and compression in these structures.

The following questions will help to elucidate the aesthetic qualities of the student work:

◆ Did you have a design or shape in mind before you started or did it evolve as you worked?

◆ What pleases you most about the design of your structure? Why?

◆ What other structures or places does your structure bring to mind?

◆ What kind of feelings does your structure evoke? Does it suggest peace, tension, humor, or excitement?

◆ Talk about how the use of balance and movement affects the feel of the structure.

◆ Pick a good name for your structure.

Finally, ask your students about how building on this scale was different from their experience on a smaller scale. How was it the same? For more on this, see the *Effect of Scale on Structure* section.

What's Going On

When building on this scale, the physical phenomena are more clearly seen and discussed. For example, the superior strength of the triangle and the need for diagonal bracing become easily apparent. Tension, compression, and twisting forces become obvious. During the building process, balance and stability are constant challenges, and students resolve these problems in a variety of interesting ways. The relative strength and weakness of the building material is revealed through this challenging building experience.

In addition, students develop an intuitive sense of how weight and strength of materials compare at this large scale. When you scale up, as in this activity, weight increases more than strength so everything seems flimsy. Also, the centers-of-mass of components are farther from attachment points, making the torques increase even more. For more discussion of these scaling effects, see the overview of *The Effect of Scale on Structure* and the overview of *The Physics and Engineering of Structure* for further details.

Extensions

◆ You can extend this activity by having students build structures of varying dimensions and with various parameters on the type and number of connectors.

BUILDING OUT

Building out means making structures where most of the weight is located out and away from the point of support. Bridges (with support at two ends) and cantilevers (with support at only one end) are structures of this type. Building out emphasizes the concepts of distribution of weight (torques) and balancing points (centers-of-mass).

Building out presents a greater challenge than building up since it involves supporting weight which is not directly over a base. There are a number of advantages to using the same materials that your students have already used to build up. First, students will benefit from the familiarity with and knowledge of the materials which they have gained in earlier building. Second, they can compare the challenges of building up with those of building out without the complication of a different material. This helps the students focus more directly on structural ideas.

A number and variety of bridge- and cantilever-building experiences are necessary to give sufficient breadth for students to develop an understanding of these structures. Students also find them to be great fun.

While you are teaching the unit, you can make the connection to students' out-of-school experiences even stronger if you and your class make an outing to look at examples of bridges and cantilevers.

Straws and Pins—Building Out

TIME

- 45-minute free exploration session if students are unfamiliar with these materials
- At least 1 hour for challenge activity

PREPARATION

- Separate the materials into packets for each individual or group.

GROUPING

- Individuals or pairs

MATERIALS
(per pair)

- 50 plastic straws
- 50 straight pins or paper clips
- 1 or 2 feet of strong tape (e.g., duct tape)
- Scissors, for cutting straws
- 10 weights (e.g., large washers or film canisters filled with sand)
- Yardstick or meterstick (can be shared by groups)

TEACHER TIPS

- Use pins only if you think it's safe. Talk about pin safety and rules for working with pins. Rules might include no traveling with the pins, or that the pins must stay on the tables or in the straws. Warn students about pricking their fingers.
- Have students take the paper off straws the day before—they'll then be curious about the upcoming activity.

Context

Building out with straws and pins provides students the opportunity to experience many of the basic physics and engineering concepts inherent in structures. Building out means that most of the structure's weight is out and away from the point of support. Bridges (with support at two ends) and cantilevers (with support at only one end) are two straightforward examples of these types of structures. Building out emphasizes experience with the concepts of torque (the combination of force and distance from a pivot point) and center-of-mass (the balance point). See the overview of *The Physics and Engineering of Structure* for details.

This activity provides a good opportunity to ask students to talk about bridges and cantilevers that they know. There are many bridges around to talk about. They range from monuments like the Golden Gate or Brooklyn bridges to simple logs thrown across a creek. Examples of cantilevers include balconies, awnings hanging in front of buildings, branches on trees, or even our arms when we hold them out. Discussion of examples like these invite your students to bring their own experience into the understanding of building out.

What It Is

If these are new materials, it is important to give your students time to freely explore with the straws and pins. Ask your students, "What can you build with 50 straws and 50 pins?" and let the students explore their ideas. Some teachers prefer to use straws and paper clips to avoid problems of getting stuck by pins, especially with younger students. However, building out (particularly cantilevers) is a good deal more difficult with paper clips. As their structures begin to take shape, suggest that they use bent paper clips as hangers for weights to test the physical strength of the structures.

After the free exploration, perhaps at the second session, pose the following challenges, using 50 straws and 50 pins:

Bridges

- Build a bridge from one desk to another. How much weight will the bridge hold?

- What's the greatest distance you can span?

- What is the strongest bridge you can build between two desks? What is the longest bridge you can build between two desks?

Cantilevers

Start with one straw taped to the wall or tabletop with strong tape. Other straws may be pinned (or fastened with clips) to this straw and may rest against the wall or tabletop but may not be taped.

- How far out from the wall or tabletop can you build a structure?

- What is the strongest cantilever you can build 18 inches out from a wall or tabletop?

The question of rules and what is fair inevitably arises in these challenges. This is an important question, as it forms the basis for scientific objectivity and fair testing.

For the bridges, questions such as, "Can you anchor the ends?" "What kind of supports can you put between the ends?" and "Where is it fair to put the weights?" often arise. You may want to define some of these rules ahead of time. For instance, you might tell students that they can't anchor the ends of their bridges and that intermediate supports cannot touch the ground. Leaving these rules to later discussion might leave some students feeling like they were cheated. On the other hand, having the students discuss and decide where and how it is fair to place weights leads to important thinking about stresses and torques on their structures.

For building out from the wall or tabletop, questions such as, "Are the structures allowed to droop, and if so, how much?" and "Where is it fair to hang the weights?" often arise. The place where weights are hung is even more important for cantilevers. When we hear students protest "it's not fair" when a group hangs their weight in close to the wall or table, we know that they have a key part in the understanding of torque; that is, that the effect depends on the distance of the weight from the pivot.

During the building process, the students should be encouraged to test the strength, stability, and durability of the structures they are working on. At the end of the building process, students should have the opportunity to observe and discuss each other's structures. For challenges involving strength, hang weights to test the strength of each structure one by one, so that the students as a class can observe what works and what doesn't work.

Discussing Results

Have the students share their results of free exploration with the whole class. Record their discoveries and questions on the chalkboard or chart paper.

In the challenge activities, issues of winners and losers may arise. Look for various criteria to judge buildings, including the degree of risk, dimension, and stability. The smallest structure may be the most stable, the most innovative may have collapsed early on. Emphasize what lessons were learned from each structure.

During testing with weights, questions like the following can help the students see some of the implications of what they are doing:

◆ How many weights can be hung before the structure collapses?

◆ Does it matter where the weights are hung?

◆ Will the structure be more likely to collapse if the weights are hung in one place or spread out?

◆ Predict where you think the structure will weaken first. Can that area be strengthened so that another area will collapse first?

In discussing any structure, special attention should be paid to structural elements that worked well or that the students learned to avoid. Attention should be directed to how individual structures change from near the support points to far from the support points.

What kind of problems did the students run into and how did they solve them? Often when building out, especially with cantilevers, the problem of twisting to one side or the other arises. Look for this problem and ask students how they dealt with it.

Look for tension and compression elements in these structures. Often, a long line of straws at the top of a structure will be in tension and a long line of straws along the bottom will be in compression.

What's Going On

If you were hanging from a tree branch with a hungry bear below you, would you be better off near the tree trunk or at the end of the branch? From these experiments, you probably know that if you're dangling from the end of the branch, the branch is more likely to droop and possibly break off, leaving you at the mercy of the bear. You can see this in your experiments with straws. Specifically, if you pin a bundle of ten straws to a single straw and hang it off the edge of a table, you will see that the ten straws will be supported. However, if you pin those ten straws end-to-end to your single straw and hang it off the edge of a table, the ten straws will droop considerably. The weight of the ten straws has not changed. But considered as a whole, the weight of the straws is farther away from the supporting edge of the table. Another way of saying this is that the center-of-mass has moved farther from the table's edge. This combination of weight and distance is called *torque*. (See the overview of *The Physics and Engineering of Structure* for more information.)

All structural action consists of tension and/or compression. In these structures, this means that every straw is either in tension or compression. It is interesting to go through a few structures with your students to try to figure out which straws are in tension and which are in compression. You can determine if you are correct by pulling out a pin on one end of the straw. If the two points where the ends of the straw had been attached move apart, the straw was under tension. If the two points move toward each other, the straw was under compression. It is interesting to compare where the tension and compression elements are in bridges versus cantilevers. In bridges, which are supported (held up) at both ends, the line of straws along the top are in compression and the line of straws along the bottom are in tension. In cantilevers, which are supported (held up) at one end, the opposite is true. Here, the line of straws along the top are in tension and the line of straws along the bottom are in compression.

Many engineering principles emerge from these activities. Your students will readily volunteer that "triangles are strong," and you will most likely see examples of diagonal bracing put in to stabilize square sections. Pin joints are common in real structures. For instance, rivets are used with steel beams and nails are used with wood planks in the same way that pins are used with straws in this activity.

Extensions

♦ Students should be encouraged to test the strength, stability, and durability of their structures. In this way, they gain insights into the behavior of structures that are subjected to outside forces, and they can see how to improve their structures so as to strengthen weak points. In addition to hanging weights on structures, they can be "wind tested" using a large piece of cardboard as a fan. You can also leave the structures intact overnight, to discover which ones are still standing in the morning.

♦ An additional interesting extension is a search for unnecessary straws. Ask the builders if they think there is a straw they could cut that would not make the whole thing fall down. Have them try it. If it works, could they cut another straw? How many cuts do they think it will take before the structure collapses? Could they build a structure that could not stand many cuts?

♦ Have the students take a set of materials home to build a structure with their family. They can draw or photograph their structure and write about what they did.

Clay Bridges

TIME

◆ 20–40 minutes

PREPARATION

◆ Set out materials.

GROUPING

◆ Pairs or individuals

MATERIALS
(per pair or individual)

◆ 8 oz. plasticene (modeling clay)
◆ Yardstick or meterstick

TEACHER TIPS

◆ Plasticene is an oil-based clay. It leaves an oily residue on surfaces. Work on paper and/or be prepared to clean tables with soap or other grease remover.

Context

Students explore the effects of gravity and weight on horizontal structures. By using the same amount of materials as in the vertical *Clay Towers* activity, students can compare and contrast vertical and horizontal building. Given the plastic (stretchy) nature of the clay, the forces of tension are particularly evident.

What It Is

Ask the students to build a bridge which

◆ spans a 6-inch gap between two tables, books, or desks

◆ supports its own weight

◆ is not anchored to the ground or tables by any other material.

If you have already done the *Clay Towers* activity, to begin this one you might raise questions referring back to the earlier activity. You could have students discuss these questions with partners or in small groups before you have a whole-group discussion. If students have been keeping science logs, have them refer back for information. Sample questions include:

◆ What kinds of things did you learn about building with clay from building clay towers?

◆ What difficulties did you face when trying to make long bridges? How did you overcome them?

◆ Do you think that you can make a bridge with the same amount of clay?

Have the students begin to build their bridges; when they complete their bridges, ask them if they could build even longer ones. How long do they think that they could make it? Have them try to build these longer bridges.

Have the students record the lengths and shapes of the bridges on chart paper so that they will have a record of the class efforts.

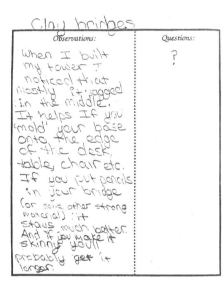

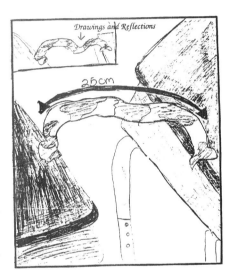

Discussing Results

Have the students talk about what was successful and what was difficult. Ask them to compare the form of a clay bridge to that of a steel bridge. The following questions may be useful in sparking discussions:

◆ How did you begin to build?

◆ What did you do to "anchor" the ends of the bridge to the table?

◆ How did you keep it from sagging?

◆ Did you think that it would fall? Why?

◆ How did it collapse? Where was it weak/strong?

◆ Does there seem to be a maximum length for this material?

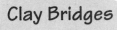

Clay Bridges

What's Going On

In building bridges, students can observe the effects of the weight of structure itself, as well as the effects of other forces acting on the structure. As the structure is lengthened, anchoring the ends (without using anything other than plasticene) can become a problem; students can observe tension and compression where the clay meets the edges of the tables.

Extensions

◆ Try building bridges with more or less clay. How does this change the structures' strength? Does this affect how long you can make a bridge?

◆ See *Toothpicks and Clay* and other bridge-building activities.

Paper Bridges

TIME

◆ 40-minute exploration
◆ 20-minute discussion

PREPARATION

◆ Collect $8\frac{1}{2}$-by-11-inch scrap paper.
◆ Set out materials.

GROUPINGS

◆ Pairs or small groups

MATERIALS

(per pair or group)

◆ 5 sheets of paper
◆ Box of large paper clips
◆ Small weights, including pennies, film canisters filled with sand, etc.
◆ Yardstick or meterstick
◆ Optional: 1 scale for the entire class

Context

Building with inherently weak materials like paper quickly leads to a close consideration of the structural elements and properties of materials. There is an element of surprise, which increases student interest in the physics, when they discover just how strong they can make this seemingly flimsy material. This activity is easily set up and gives students a chance to explore the material as a lead-in to further building. It can be done on its own or as a lead-in or follow-up to the *Building with Newspaper* activities. Building bridges emphasizes the concepts involved in carrying weight at a distance from the supports. See the overview of *The Physics and Engineering of Structure* for more details.

This activity provides a good opportunity to ask students to talk about bridges and cantilevers that they know. There are many bridges around to talk about. They range from monuments like the Golden Gate or Brooklyn bridges to simple logs thrown across a creek. Examples of cantilevers include balconies, awnings hanging in front of buildings, branches on trees, or even our arms when we hold them out. Discussion of examples like these invite your students to bring their own experience into the understanding of building out.

What It Is

Ask the students to take a sheet of paper and construct a bridge which will span an 8-inch gap between desks. They should not use any materials to anchor the bridge to the desks.

When the students have achieved this first step, ask them to experiment by adding small weights, one at a time, to the center of the bridge. When their bridge collapses, have the students try to construct an even stronger bridge, using another sheet of paper.

Keep a record of the trials. Ask the students to draw the shape of their bridge and mark down how much weight each bridge held before collapsing. In addition to having them write down "five pennies" or "three paper clips," have the students measure the weights of the pennies, paper clips, or whatevers, on a scale, and record the loads on the bridges. Have the students draw a cross-section of their bridges, as well as a silhouette, so that they will be able to look closely at which constructions were successful and which were not.

Discussing Results

Have the students share their particularly strong or weak bridges with the rest of the class. Discuss and chart the shapes which were discovered to be successful. Ask the following questions:

* What shape seemed to be the weakest/strongest?

* What part of the bridge seemed to collapse first?

* Where was the bridge weakest?

* What would you use to make the paper bridge even stronger?

* What do you think would happen if the desks were farther apart? closer together? Why?

* What do you think would happen if you could anchor the bridges to the desks? Why?

What's Going On

Many of the major concepts from the overview of *The Physics and Engineering of Structure* are encountered in this activity. Bridges especially illustrate the effect of weight or another force at a distance from a pivot or support point (torque), and they also provide experience with beams.

In this activity, students experiment with a variety of shapes such as folded corrugations and rolled tubes that can make an inherently weak material such as paper much stronger. Paper is very weak under compression and is somewhat stronger under tension (i.e., it collapses when you push the ends together but it doesn't pull apart easily). When you put weight on a sheet of paper it tends to buckle because it is very thin. It has no strength along the thin direction. By folding or rolling the paper, you create a "thickness" which allows the paper to reinforce itself and not collapse so easily.

You can illustrate this property of paper in a simple demonstration with an 8-foot-long 2-by-4 piece of lumber. Support the beam on two short blocks at either end. Lay the beam flat and push down at the center. It gives easily. Now, turn the beam on its side (have helpers steady each end on the blocks for stability). In this case, when you push down at the center, the beam is much more rigid. When turned on its side, there is more wood further from the center line, in

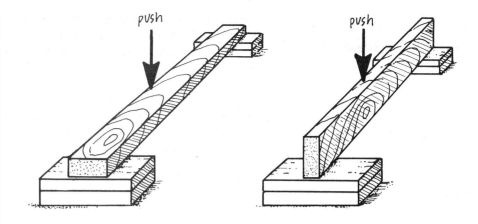

the areas where it can best counteract the tension on the top and compression on the bottom.

In construction with steel beams, I beams are used just for this reason; to put most of the steel where the greatest stress is experienced. In the paper construction, rolled tubes of paper prove to be very strong. Again, most of the paper here is put on the edges where the stresses are greater. See the overview of *The Physics and Engineering of Structure* on beams for more on this.

Extensions

◆ Other paper-building activities and testing can extend this work. Can you build a paper column that will support a book? Can you build a strong paper wall? Design a test to find the strongest paper beam. All of these questions look at the interplay between properties of the material (paper) and form.

◆ Building paper bridges with other kinds of paper can also extend this work. What can you do with a single sheet of newspaper? How about a sheet of tissue paper? What can you build with a sheet of tagboard?

Garden Poles— Building Out

Time

- Several 1–2 hour sessions
- Final session may take up to half a day.

Preparation

- Bundle poles and tape for each group.
- Reserve a large space, like part of a playground or cafeteria, for both building and storing between sessions.

Grouping

- Four or five per group

Materials
(per group)

- 35 4-foot bamboo garden stakes
- One roll of $\frac{3}{4}$-inch masking tape
- 3–6 feet of duct tape
- Matte knives or scissors
- Optional: 25 weights to be shared by several groups (e.g., large washers or film canisters filled with sand)

Teacher Tips

- You'll need a lot of space for construction and collapse.
- Pictures help to record student efforts and make the deconstruction of their structures less dramatic.
- Use matte knives or scissors to take apart the structures.

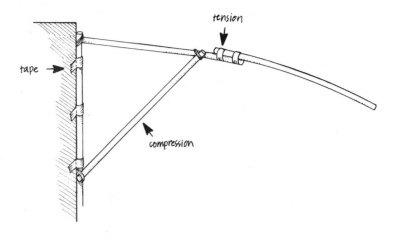

Context

Building out with garden poles and tape provides students with the opportunity to experience the same basic physics and engineering phenomena as they encountered in smaller-scale activities such as *Straws and Pins—Building Out.* Students will have an entirely different experience of these phenomena due to the changes caused by the change of scale. Materials seem more flimsy, joints seem less secure. This is a good activity to do near the end of your structure and scale unit, and should be preceded by building on a smaller scale. As in the smaller scale building-out activities, students should be given the opportunity to talk about bridges and cantilever structures that they know.

Building on this scale provides a perfect opportunity to discuss the students' different experiences of building activities at different scales. For more discussion of this, see the *Effect of Scale on Structure* section.

What It Is

Working with these materials may be very different from other building that they have done. The students need an initial session where they can familiarize themselves with these materials, as building out is particularly difficult on this scale. If this is your students' first use of garden poles and tape, the first session should aim at simply establishing familiarity with these materials. In this session, ask the students to build a self-standing structure using 35 bamboo garden poles and masking tape. Give them the following rules for construction:

◆ The tape can only be wrapped twice around any given joint or stick.

◆ When joining sticks in a straight line, the sticks may only be taped together at two points (at each of these points, the piece of tape may only be wrapped around twice).

garden poles taped together in two spots

At the end of the session, record their accomplishments through video or photography or by having the students draw pictures of their structures. Then have the students deconstruct the materials so that they can be used again at the next session.

For the next session, introduce the cantilever. A cantilever is a projecting beam or other structure which is supported at only one end (e.g., awnings, flagpoles, tree limbs). Challenge your students to build a cantilever out from a wall or out from a tabletop. Use the same rules for building as above with the following addition:

◆ Sticks may be taped to the wall, fence, or tabletop with a reasonable amount of duct tape.

Challenge the students to do one of the following:

◆ With 35 garden stakes, how far out from the wall or tabletop can you build a structure?

◆ Can you build a cantilever 11 feet out from the wall or tabletop?

◆ What is the strongest cantilever you can build 7 feet out from a wall or tabletop?

◆ Can you build a cantilever 9 feet out from the wall or tabletop that will hold one film canister of sand?

Choose or adjust the difficulty of the challenge based on the age and level of building skills of your students.

The question of rules and what is fair inevitably arises in these challenges. Questions such as, "Are the structures allowed to droop, and if so, how much?" and "How do you measure distance from the wall or tabletop?" almost always come up for these cantilevers. Setting these rules by class discussion enhances sensitivity to these problems. "Where is it fair to hang the weights?" is another question that often arises. The place where weights are hung is critical for cantilevers. When we hear students protest "it's not fair" when a group hangs their weight in close to the wall or table, we know that they have understood an important aspect of torque.

During the building process, students should be encouraged to test the strength, stability, and durability of the structures they are constructing. At the end of the building process, students should have the opportunity to observe and discuss each other's structures. For challenges involving strength, hang weights to test the strength of each structure one by one, so that the students as a class can observe what works and what doesn't.

Aesthetics is a particularly important criterion for these structures. Aesthetics is not just how pretty a structure is, but also how it makes the observer feel. Is the structure rigid and strong looking? Does it have a pleasing curve to it? Is it open, light, and airy? Does it create a feeling of tension, as if something is about to happen? Does it create an image of movement? These garden pole structures may be considered sculptures and looked at in those terms.

Discussing Results

After the initial session, have the students share their free exploration results with the whole class. Record their discoveries on the chalkboard or chart paper; students may also record drawings of structures, observations, and questions in science logs.

- ◆ What did they experience and discover while building?

- ◆ What difficulties did they encounter and how did they resolve them?

- ◆ What questions do they have as a result of the activity?

- ◆ What would they change if they were to build it again?

The final building session is followed by weight testing, measurement, and discussion.

- ◆ What did they observe happening?

- ◆ If their structure was wobbly, how did they stabilize it?

Often when building cantilevers, the problem of sideways twisting arises. These large-scale cantilevers are very susceptible to this, and many have a strong tendency to do anything but stay straight. Look for these challenges and ask students how they dealt with it.

Most of these cantilever structures will not hold much weight. In structures that are tested with weights, raising questions like the following can help the students see some of the implications of what they are doing:

- ◆ How many weights can be hung before the structure collapses?

- ◆ Does it matter where the weights are hung?

- ◆ Will the structure be more likely to collapse if the weights are hung in one place or spread out?

- ◆ Predict where you think the structure will weaken first. Can that area be strengthened so that another area will collapse first?

Questions about which poles are being bent and where poles are being pulled out of their taped joints help locate the tension and compression elements in these structures. Often, a long line of poles at the top of a structure will be in tension and a long line of poles along the bottom will be in compression.

Finally, ask your students about how building on this scale differs from their experience on a smaller scale. How is it the same? For more on this, see the *Effect of Scale on Structure* section.

What's Going On

In building on this scale, the physics phenomena are more clearly seen and discussed. For example, the superior strength of the triangle and need for diagonal bracing becomes easily apparent. Tension, compression, and the effect of weight at a distance from its support (torque) become very obvious. During the building process, balance and stability are constantly challenged, and students resolve these problems in a variety of interesting ways. The relative strength and weakness of the building material is revealed through this challenging building experience.

In addition, students develop an intuitive sense of how the weight and strength of materials compare at this large scale. When you scale up, as in this activity, weights increase more than strength so everything seems flimsy. When working on this scale, the center-of-mass of the cantilevers gets far away from the supporting wall or table very rapidly. This creates much greater torque on the cantilevers, causing a great tendency toward twisting and turning. For more discussion of these scaling effects, see the *Effect of Scale on Structure* section.

Extensions

◆ You can extend this activity by having students build structures of varying dimensions and with various parameters on the type and number of connectors.

BUILDING WITH NEWSPAPER

Newspaper has proven to be a great medium for classroom building because it reveals a number of structural principles. It is also readily available and relatively cheap and is a material with which students are already familiar.

Students know newspaper as something that is weak and floppy. Building with newspaper provides an engaging element of surprise. Students become delighted that through their ideas and efforts, they can make this flimsy material into something strong and stable. (One group of sixth-grade girls even constructed a chair on which they could sit.)

The following three activities are designed to develop in progression student understanding of both the materials and their efficient use, leading to the construction of a bridge that will bear a significant load. The first activity focuses simply on making the weak material strong. It provides the critical "messing around" time for becoming acquainted with a new material. The second activity focuses on the engineering ideas surrounding the joining of materials. If you do not want to focus on joints, this activity may be skipped. Some teachers combine the first and second activities into a single activity by choosing only one joining material, such as masking tape. Students then may explore strengthening newspaper and joining pieces at the same time.

The third activity provides an opportunity for students to apply what they have learned about the materials in the previous activity to the challenge of building a bridge. They are invariably surprised and delighted with just how much weight their bridges can hold.

Building with Newspaper I

Exploring Materials

Time

- ◆ 40–60 minutes to build
- ◆ 40 minutes total for both introductory and follow-up discussion

Preparation

- ◆ Set out materials.

Grouping

- ◆ Pairs

Materials
(per pair)

- ◆ At least 15 sheets of newspaper
- ◆ Optional: 2-inch tape
- ◆ Optional: Small weights (e.g., film canisters filled with sand) and hangers (e.g., string, wire, or paper clips) to test the strength of the paper constructions

Context

Building with inherently weak or flimsy materials brings students to look closely at the nature of that material. Students can then explore the relationships between the material and the shape, stability, and strength of the structure built with that material.

This activity can be done early in the unit, with emphasis on the structural aspects; or it can be done later, with emphasis on the effects of scale on structure.

What It Is

Begin with a class brainstorm about structure. Have students discuss their ideas about both natural and human-made structures. You may want to share books about or photos of various structures.

Then continue with simple questions, such as:

◆ What can you build with newspaper?

◆ How can you make newspaper strong?

Students explore ways that the newspaper can be strengthened, lengthened, and connected. They may invent techniques such as folding, twisting, rolling, looping, overlapping, or crumpling to strengthen the material (especially if tape is not being used).

After their constructions are completed, the students may test the strength of their work by hanging or placing weights on their newspaper structures. This will generally challenge the students to make their constructions even stronger.

Discussing Results

After the activity, students share their results with the whole class. Structures should be available to illustrate the ideas that the students discuss. Their discoveries can be written down on the chalkboard/chart paper and/or recorded individually in science logs for future reference. You and the students can make two different lists: "Observations" and "Questions." These records should be available (posted, if on charts) for future reference.

The following questions have proven useful in extending discussion:

◆ What were you trying to do? Did you have a plan? Did it change as you began to build?

◆ What problems did you run into? How did you solve them?

◆ What worked? What didn't work?

◆ What was surprising?

◆ Have you seen anything in the outside world that reminds you of your structure? How are they similar?

The following questions have served as good lead-ins to the next activity:

◆ How do you think you could make a bigger version?

◆ What do you think you could do with another material (e.g., construction paper or cardboard)?

◆ What could you do to make your structure even stronger?

What's Going On

In this activity, students experiment with the variety of shapes, such as folded corrugations and rolled tubes, that can make an inherently weak material such as newspaper much stronger. Newspaper is very weak under compression and is somewhat stronger under tension (i.e., it collapses when you push the ends together but it doesn't pull apart easily). When you put weight on a sheet of newspaper it tends to buckle because it is very thin. It has no strength along the thin direction. By folding or rolling the newspaper, you create a "thickness" which allows the newspaper to reinforce itself and not collapse so easily.

You can illustrate this property of paper in a simple demonstration with an 8-foot-long 2-by-4 piece of lumber. Support the 2-by-4 on two short blocks at either end. Lay the 2-by-4 flat and push down at the center. It gives easily. Now, turn the 2-by-4 on its side (have helpers steady each end on the blocks for stability). In this case, when you push down at the center, the 2-by-4 is much more rigid. When turned on its side, there is more wood further from the center line, in the areas where it can best counteract the tension on the top and compression on the bottom. In construction with steel beams, I beams are used for just this reason—to put most of the steel where the greatest stress is experienced.

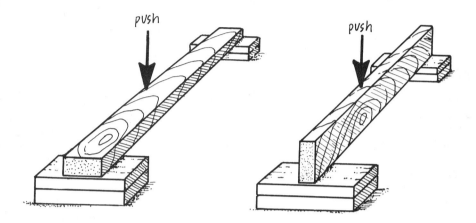

Many students will find that they can overcome the floppy, weak nature of the newspaper by rolling it into tubes and using the tubes as their building blocks. Tubes are a very efficient structural component. They put the bulk of the material away from the center line, close to the edges where it is needed to overcome the tension and compression of bending. The layers of newspaper formed by stacked tubes serve as reinforcement. See the overview of *The Physics and Engineering of Structure* on beams and columns for more details.

Extensions

♦ See *Building with Newspaper II* and *III*.

Building with Newspaper II

Exploring Joints

TIME

- ◆ 40–60 minutes to build
- ◆ 40–60 minutes total for both introductory and follow-up discussion

PREPARATION

- ◆ Set out materials.

GROUPING

- ◆ Pairs

MATERIALS
(per pair)

- ◆ About 45 sheets of newspaper
- ◆ One type of connector for each group (e.g., 3-foot lengths of masking tape, glue, 6-foot lengths of string, 30 paper clips, 20 pipe cleaners, or 3-foot lengths of wire)
- ◆ Optional: Small weights found in the classroom (pens, erasers, blocks, etc.)

TEACHER TIPS

- ◆ Have students bring connectors from home.
- ◆ For comparison in follow-up discussion, have at least two types of connectors being used in the classroom.

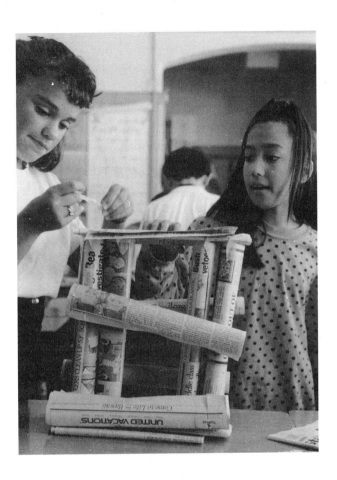

Context

All construction is accomplished by using connectors to combine materials of limited size. These connectors can be nails, which combine pieces of wood; rivets and welds, which combine pieces of metal; or cartilage, which combines pieces of bone. The type and placement of the connector determines the strength, flexibility, and utility of the joint, and therefore of the entire structure. This activity provides a good opportunity to ask students to talk about joints and connectors in structures that they know. These include such everyday types as glue, staples, buttons, and snaps. Discussion of examples like these invite your students to bring their own experience into the understanding of building out.

The objective of this activity is to use connectors to make a construction stronger or larger than it would have been if connectors had not been used.

Exploring the use of connectors extends the *Building with Newspapers I* activity and prepares students for further construction experience.

What It Is

In this activity each group uses only one type of connector in limited amounts.

Begin the activity by discussing what a joint is and how it is useful to an object. Students may want to look at their desks and note the use of screws and bolts. How has using these connectors made their desks stronger? What is the utility of their wrist joints? Would their hands be more agile without wrists? Discuss the concepts of a joint that provides flexibility (a wrist) and a joint that provides strength/reinforcement (a bolt in a desk). When is one used over another?

As in the first activity, students should be allowed to create any type of construction they wish, with the idea that by using connectors, they can create a stronger or bigger structure. Students who work with reinforcement-type connectors (such as glue) will be more likely to build rigid structures, whereas students who work with flexible connectors (such as tape) will probably build structures which can adjust to the addition of weight and size.

Students may want to test their work by adding weights found in the classroom.

Discussing Results

Many of the same questions from the first activity can be used here. In addition, the following questions may prove useful:

- Is your structure stronger as a column (vertical) or as a beam (horizontal)?
- What is the difference between working with connectors and working without them?
- How did you use your connector in different ways?
- What is similar and what is different in using different connectors?

What's Going On

The problem of joining pieces comes up in this activity. Joints tend to be points about which structural elements can pivot. But if all of the building elements can pivot on the joints, the structure will collapse. You see this in square or rectangular sections which have a strong tendency to collapse. To prevent collapse and maintain structural shape, you must make rigid sections. This can be done by building with triangles and using cross-braces which create triangular sections.

Some connectors (like glue) make quite strong and rigid joints, much like welded joints in metal or glue joints in wooden structures. However, these joints are inflexible and can't adjust or move to redistribute a load. Some connectors (like tape or string) allow the joint to pivot. For more rigid connections, two of these second types of connectors must be spaced apart, for reinforcement.

Extensions

◆ Welded, glued, nailed, screwed, riveted, and sewn joints are all around us. You can compare the similarities and differences in such joints with the ones made in this activity. Have your students identify the joints they see around them and discuss why that particular connector might have been used.

◆ See also *Building with Newspaper III.*

Building with Newspaper III

Newspaper Bridges

TIME

- Two or three 40–60 minute building sessions
- 20–60 minutes of introductory and follow-up discussion at each session (more at the last session)

PREPARATION

- Set out materials.
- Find a roomy space to store unfinished bridges.

GROUPING

- Three to four per group

MATERIALS
(per group)

- A lot of newspaper (2–4 Sunday papers)
- 6-foot length of tape (or string or yarn or rubber bands)
- Several identical heavy objects (such as textbooks) for weights
- Optional: bathroom or other scale

Context

In this activity, students will begin to develop an experiential understanding of how structures are designed to bear loads, or downward pulls. Much of the groundwork will be laid for developing an understanding of the concepts discussed in the overview of *The Physics and Engineering of Structure*. Building bridges emphasizes the concepts of torques and center-of-mass by carrying weight at a distance from the supports.

This activity provides an opportunity to ask students to talk about bridges that they know. There are obvious examples such as the Golden Gate or Brooklyn bridges, but the smaller, unnoticed examples may be equally as interesting. Look for roads crossing little creeks, pedestrian overpasses, or even second-story floors in buildings. There are many resources (books, videos) on the history and construction of bridges (see Appendix B). A discussion of such examples invites students to bring their own experiences and understandings of bridges to the activity, thereby connecting their school experiences with the outside world.

What It Is

Ask the students to build a structure with newspapers and tape which

♦ spans 18 inches between two tables or chairs (have older students span 24 inches)

♦ supports the weight of one or more books

♦ is not anchored to the ground or tables by any other material.

The students will adjust and modify their bridges over several class sessions. Sometimes they will have to scrap their initial designs and start over. This often provides an opportunity to talk to students about the fact that you learn as much or more from things that do not work as from things that do work. Ideas that fail in practice can be very frustrating. It is important to recognize and acknowledge the learning that comes from these failed attempts. Ask the students to keep notes of their efforts in their journals. They will generally draw pictures and detail how their structures become stronger over time.

When the bridges are completed in the second or third session, test their strength one by one in front of the whole class. See *Discussing Results* below for ideas.

Many bridges may actually hold the weight of one or more students. Students become quite excited by the challenge of trying to hold their own weight, and this can lead to several extensions (see below).

News paper bridge-HEAVY LUMPS
AMELIA- 3rd grader

When we started making newspaper bridges, Mrs. Uyeda thought that a three½ pound dictionary would be too heavy but in the end, ours held 230 pounds! I'll tell you how it happened. First we kept on building in the middle and I sat on it, it callapsed. Then we started to build on the sides and the middle. one of the problems we had was we used so much tape that it stuck to everything. The bottom was very bumpy and it was very heavy. Thats how it got its name. After quite a bit of careful building I sat on it. It held me! Then Tyler sat on it. I held us both! At first, we did not want Annalise to sit on it because she weigh 88 pounds and me and Tyler are only 71 pounds each. But then she covinced us to let her on. It held all three of us. That was our final record. The tables that we were building across were 18 inces apart. This is what our final record looked like:

```
  88 lbs Annalise    We were in
  71 lbs Amelia      second place for
+ 71 lbs Tyler       the most weight
 230
```

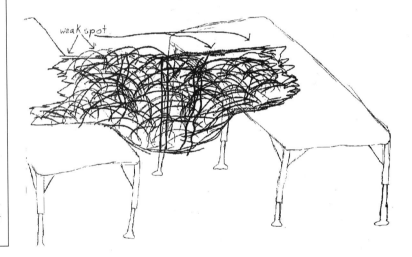

Discussing Results

Before beginning the testing, ask the following questions:

♦ How did you start building? Was there a plan or a general idea?

♦ What was your group's process of making the bridge?

♦ Did you get stuck or run into any problems? How did you overcome them?

Before testing, or during the first test, discuss what constitutes a fair test by asking how and where the weights should be placed on the bridges. Should the weight be dropped onto the bridge? Placed gently onto the bridge? If your class decides that all weight must be placed gently in the center, they are recognizing that the weight, its position, and how it is placed on the bridge may all be relevant variables in this experiment. In order to get "fair" objective results, only one variable may change (the weight), and the others (placement and position of the weight) must remain unchanged. The idea of a fair test is fundamental to the concept of scientific objectivity.

As you begin the adding of weights, the students themselves will generate many questions for discussion. They will be interested in which bridge holds the most weight, and exactly how much it holds.

Keep adding the weights to the bridge until it breaks. Questions connected with the breaking can include the following:

◆ How much weight does your bridge hold?

◆ Where does the bridge start to break? What do you think is happening?

◆ Why do you think one bridge is stronger than another?

◆ How could a bridge be made stronger?

◆ How could you build a strong bridge using less newspaper? (This question can lead to a possible follow-up activity.)

What's Going On

Building bridges demonstrates the effect of weight or another force at a distance from a pivot or a support point (torque). In addition, it makes clear the need for the upward support of the bridge to counteract the downward force of the load.

One of the clearest principles illustrated in this activity has to do with beams. If the span of the newspaper bridge is considered as a beam, the crushing and bending of the bridge under its load makes the stresses on the beam quite evident (see the beams section in the overview of *The Physics and Engineering of Structure*).

Extensions

Math

In the classroom, students become interested in exactly how much weight their bridge will hold. Students can go to the chalkboard to add together the weights of the books (or bodies) which their bridges would hold. In a fifth-grade class, the students took the weight of a book and multiplied it by the total number of books on the bridge. When they ran out of one type of textbook and had to use another, the problem became more complex.

Efficiency

One of the interesting ways to assess the bridges is to look at design efficiency. By efficiency, we mean how much newspaper it takes to hold up a pound of load. To find this, first determine the amount of newspaper used by weighing it. Then, divide the weight of the load by the weight of the bridge itself. The larger the result (load per unit amount of newspaper), the more efficient your bridge design.

Real Life

Students can look for bridges in the world around them. There are obvious examples, such as monuments like the Golden Gate, but there are many other less noticeable examples as well. Students can look for roads crossing creeks, pedestrian overpasses, or even second-story floors in their school. There are many books and videos which discuss the history and construction of bridges.

Build with Less

A natural extension of this activity is to ask the class: "What is the minimum amount of newspaper and tape that you would need to support one (or more) books?" Have the class try to build a "minimalist" bridge. This challenge should be preceded by a discussion of why one would wish to design a minimalist bridge. This could lead to discussions of "real world" considerations of cost factors in building. It also introduces a constraint that forces the students to look more closely at and apply what they have learned about what makes their bridges strong.

Balancing Acts

Balance is an underlying experience in every student's life. Discussion of what is balance or what students think makes something balanced is very useful before and after an initial exploration of materials. Students' experiences, ranging from seesaws to the experience of balance and stability in their own bodies, should be central to the discussion around this section's activities.

When building cantilevers out from a wall or a table, building bridges, or even building towers, students encounter the physics concepts of torque—"force at a distance" from a support or pivot—and center-of-mass. Examples of these fundamental physics and engineering concepts can be explored more extensively in the study of balance.

A good way to begin investigations of balance is to do several activities (e.g., *Balance Board I, Little Balance Board, Two-Dimensional Balance,* and *Three-Dimensional Balance*) in tandem as centers. When done in centers, students get the opportunity to explore aspects of balance in one, two, and three dimensions and to experience the idea of center-of-mass within many contexts in close proximity. Using centers allows students to start with a broad picture of these concepts rather than getting locked into narrow definitions. More detailed analysis can be done in later sessions.

An exploration of balance emphasizes the fact that it is not just weight that is important to take into account when building, but also the distribution of the weight. For two and three dimensions, you must also consider direction (e.g., left, right, back, forth, up, down). The combination of weight (or any other force) and distance from a support or pivot point is known as *torque*. (See the overview of *The Physics and Engineering of Structure* for a more complete discussion of torque.) To achieve balance, the sum of the torques to one side of the fulcrum (or pivot point) must equal the sum of the torques on the other side.

Many of the objects in a balanced structure do not have their mass at a single point. Their mass, and hence their weight, is spread throughout their substance. When you think about the distance and direction of the weight from the fulcrum, you could think about the distributed weight and distance, but it's easier to think about the weight as if it were all at one point. This point is known as the *center-of-mass*. See more about the center-of-mass in the overview of *The Physics and Engineering of Structure.*

Stability is another important aspect of structures that you deal with in these balance activities. The higher the weight gets above the fulcrum, the less stable the balance. *Stability* is defined here as the ability of a structure to restore its balance after it has been disturbed. Increased stability with lower centers-of-mass is an effect which is familiar to anyone who skis, skates, or snowboards. A person's center-of-mass is near the midsection. If you stand tall with legs close together (narrowing your base), you fall over easily. By bending low (lowering your center-of-mass) and spreading your legs wider (making a wider base), you can become much more stable. In this case, your center-of-mass stays over your base even as you tilt from side to side. (See the *Body Balance* activity for more on this.)

A key concept in all physical structures is that the force and torques acting on a structure must be in balance for the structure to stand. Forces pulling down (such as weight) must equal forces pushing up (such as the elastic force within the structure). Torques tending to turn the structure clockwise must be balanced by those tending to turn it counterclockwise. This concept is well illustrated by balance activities.

Four-Foot Balance Board I

TIME

- 1 hour

PREPARATION

- Make the materials.
- Set out materials.

GROUPING

- Two to four per group

MATERIALS

(per group)

- One 4-foot 1-by-4 board
- A fulcrum
- Set of blocks of about uniform density
- Assorted items to balance

TEACHER TIPS

- See *Making the Materials* inset at the end of this activity.
- This activity works well as one of several balance activities (such as *Little Balance Board, Two-Dimensional Balance,* and *Three-Dimensional Balance*) done in tandem in centers around the classroom.

Context

Balance is a central experience in every person's life. Discussion of what is balance or what students think makes something balanced is very useful before and after initial exploration of materials. With this particular activity, the seesaw is the most direct analog from the students' outside experiences and should come up in discussions.

While building out from a wall or a table (cantilevers), building bridges, and even building straight up, students encounter torque ("force at a distance" from a support or pivot) and the effects of weight distribution—concepts that can be explored more extensively in the study of balance. The balance board is the simplest case for exploring balance. Here the weights are placed somewhere along the board and can only be moved in one dimension. Torques and balance in two and three dimensions are explored in the *Two-Dimensional Balance* and *Three-Dimensional Balance* activities. The concepts explored in these activities are central to the physics and engineering of structure.

What It Is

Start the activity by discussing the materials to be used. Ask questions such as:

◆ What does the board remind you of?

◆ What do you think you can use it for?

Students will come up with ideas like seesaws, ramps, slides, etc. Allow some time for the students to play with the boards and fulcrums. After initial exploration, ask students what they think balance is. This elicits information about the students' prior knowledge and helps them start thinking about what is happening in these activities. Begin to focus their investigations by asking the following series of questions:

◆ Can you balance the 4-foot board on the fulcrum?

If the board is uniform, it should balance in the center. Knots or other irregularities may cause the board to balance slightly off-center.

◆ Can you balance the board with things on it?

With this prompt, the students will tend to begin to build on the board. Many students will try to construct high towers. To keep the board steady, they may prop it up from underneath. After completing their structures, take away the props to see if the board is balanced. Cover your ears before everything crashes to the ground.

◆ Is it possible to build on the board and keep both ends off the floor without propping it up?

Some students build symmetrically from the start. They select blocks or other weights and arrange them at the ends of the board or over the fulcrum. After pairing and balancing similar things, students may begin to try dissimilar objects. Prompts for further exploration can include, "Can unlike objects be alike in weight?" "Can you balance unlike things?"

◆ How many ways can you tip the board? What happens if you move something that's sitting on it? add something? remove something? Once you've tipped it, can you make it balanced again?

Moving an object a slight distance on the board affects the balance a great deal. This becomes obvious to students as they explore tipping the board.

Generally, you will find that the students will use very simple "weight" words to express what they are doing: "This side is heavier," "Now it's heavier on this side." Even though they do not talk about the effect of distance-from-the-pivot-point (i.e., torque), they are using and coming to terms with this idea.

◆ Experiment with moving the fulcrum (i.e., balance the board off-center). How else can you balance the board? Can you balance it with something at just one end?

When students discover that they can control the balance by moving the fulcrum, they will think of countless new possibilities to explore.

Discussing Results

When discussing the results of this activity it is useful to have a balance board in front of the classroom. You and your students can use it to physically demonstrate your questions and their answers and comments.

Ask the following questions:

◆ What discoveries did you make? (Have students demonstrate these.)

◆ What happens if you move an object farther from the fulcrum? closer to the fulcrum?

◆ What happens if you add more weight on the left? on the right?

◆ What happens if you shift the board to the right? to the left?

The observation that some arrangements of things on the board are easy to balance, some are hard to balance, and some are impossible to balance often comes up. This observation can lead to the important distinctions between balance, where all the forces and torques acting on a body are in equilibrium and the object is at rest, and stability, where a structure has the ability to restore its balance after it has been disturbed.

If students come up with conflicting observations, discuss things they could try to do to reconcile their conflicts. For instance, suppose one group of students says you can add one block on each end of the balance board without destroying the balance and another group says you can't. Have them try to resolve this disagreement by designing experiments to test the claim. They should look at when the claim works or does not work.

What's Going On

This exploration of balance emphasizes the fact that it is not just weight that is important to take into account when building, but also the distribution of the weight. The combination of weight (or any other force) and distance from a support or pivot point is known as *torque*. (See the overview of *The Physics and Engineering of Structure* for a more complete discussion of torque.) For these linear (or straight-board) balances, torque is weight times the distance from the fulcrum. To achieve balance, the sum of the torques to the right of the fulcrum must equal the sum of the torques to the left of the fulcrum.

Many of the objects put on the balance board do not have their mass at a single point. Their mass, and hence their weight, is spread throughout their substance. Imagine a large sheet of aluminum foil which has its weight distributed over its large area; if you crumpled the sheet of foil into a ball, the same weight would become concentrated in a small space. Think of the weight of that large sheet of aluminum foil as if the foil were crumpled into a ball around the center point of the sheet of foil. This point is known as the *center-of-mass*. In this board activity, when you think about the distance of the weight from the fulcrum, you could think about the distributed weight and distance of the balancing objects (as with the large sheet of foil), but it's easier to think about the weight as if it were all at one point (as in the crumpled ball of foil). See more about the center-of-mass in the overview of *The Physics and Engineering of Structure*.

Students will often build on the balance board. As they build higher and higher, the balance gets less and less stable. (*Stability* is defined here as the ability of a structure to restore its balance after it has been disturbed.) This is because as the building grows upward, the weight being balanced, and hence its center-of-mass, moves higher in relation to the fulcrum. When the center-of-mass is high, a small shift in the balance board can move it out horizontally, away from the line directly over the fulcrum. When the center-of-mass is lower, the same slight shift does not move it nearly as far horizontally.

The rounded fulcrums used in this activity give the balancing board and blocks a means of self-correction, enabling it to find the exact balance point. While building on the board, if you shift a weight or tip the board, the board can tilt, changing the point where the board touches the fulcrum and adjusting the balance. But if the weight is too high, a slight tilt of the board will take it out of the range for self-adjustment and destroy stability.

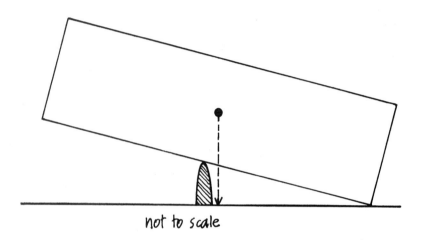

not to scale

Increased stability with lower centers-of-mass is an effect which is familiar to anyone who skis, skates, or snowboards. A person's center-of-mass is near the midsection. If you stand tall with legs close together (narrowing your base), you fall over easily. By bending low (lowering your center-of-mass) and spreading your legs wider (making a wider base), you can become much more stable. In this case, your center-of-mass stays over your base even as you tilt from side to side. (See the *Body Balance* activity for more on this.)

Extensions

See *Four-Foot Balance Board II*.

Making the Materials

Fulcrums—You can make a fulcrum by taking a 4-inch length of mailing tube and cutting it in half lengthwise. You can also take a piece of tube or pipe about 5 inches long and tape it to a wooden base. Alternatively, you can use two pieces of clay to stabilize the tube.

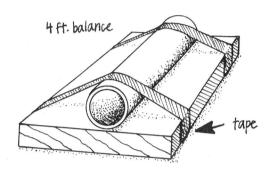

Blocks—You can make blocks out of 2-by-2 or 2-by-4 lumber. The cheapest method is to get scraps from lumber yards, construction sites, or contractors. Cut pieces about $2\frac{1}{2}$ inches long and 5 inches long. Or go to a lumber yard and ask them to cut a set to size for you. If available, unit blocks also make great weights.

Balancing Materials—Anything of manageable size will do. You can use cans of food, containers of dry food, books, bricks, shoes, and/or sand in containers.

Four-Foot Balance Board II

TIME

◆ 1 hour

PREPARATION

◆ Construct boards, fulcrums, and blocks in advance.
◆ Set up materials for easy distribution to groups.

GROUPING

◆ Two to four per group

MATERIALS
(per group)

◆ One 4-foot 1-by-4 board
◆ A fulcrum
◆ Set of blocks of about uniform weight or multiples of a unit weight

TEACHER TIPS

◆ See previous activity for how to construct the materials.

Context

This activity allows for more systematic experimentation than possible in the *Four-Foot Balance Board I* activity. Since the blocks used here contain units of about equal weight and their multiples, students can consider just one variable: the distance of the blocks from the fulcrum. Possible questions and activities with the blocks are given below. They are samples only, and are more numerous than any one class would be likely to pursue. However, by studying them, you may be able to anticipate some of the promising avenues for student learning, as well as help clarify the problems your class confronts.

What It Is

Exploration with these materials can be initiated and extended by asking some of the following questions:

- Where do you think blocks of equal weight can be placed on a balanced board without disturbing the balance? (The students may find a variety of positions; some of them may come up with a general rule. Students may place a block on each end or they may place a block 1 foot to the left of the fulcrum and a block 1 foot to the right.)

- Where can additional pairs of blocks that are equal in weight be added to a balance board without disturbing the balance? Try four blocks. Try six. Can the students find a rule?

- Try the reverse: Which blocks can be removed without unbalancing the board? Can you remove single blocks or do you need to remove pairs or more? Try putting a number of blocks on the board and then balancing the board on the fulcrum. Now try removing blocks and maintaining the balance.

Working with an odd number of blocks—for instance, three blocks—ask the following three questions:

- How can you balance the board with three blocks of equal weight? (One solution is to place one block over the fulcrum and the other two at opposite ends. Students might point out that the block over the fulcrum isn't "balancing anything" and can be taken off.)

- If you place a single block at an end of the board, where will the two other blocks go?

- Try balancing the board with one block not resting over the fulcrum. Now try adding blocks to the off-center board.

Other challenges to pose to the students include:

- Try to move blocks on a balance board without destroying the balance. (It's often surprising to find that, once balanced, the board will stay that way when blocks are moved to new positions. Some work; others don't. When students get the idea that the system is predictable, they enjoy playing games with it. The object is to make changes and have the board balanced after a move. One student holds the board while the partner makes the moves.)

- Try to turn blocks on a balanced board and still maintain the balance. You can rotate blocks sideways or turn them on end. Can you pile blocks up? (A block can be turned to any position without affecting the balance, so long as the center of the block remains the same distance from the fulcrum.)

Discussing Results

Have the students discuss what they were trying to find out and any unexpected discoveries they made. Direct specific questions to the prompts you used at the beginning or during the activity. For example, if you asked, "Can you move blocks on a balanced board without destroying the balance?" ask if they found any patterns to moves that worked or didn't work.

These materials lend themselves to more systematic results. Ask if they found any patterns or rules in their investigations.

What's Going On

This more systematic exploration of balance emphasizes the balancing of torques along a straight line (in one dimension). Torque is the combination of weight (or any other force) and distance from a support or pivot point. (See the overview of *The Physics and Engineering of Structure* for a more complete discussion of torque.) Formally, for these balances, torque is weight times the distance from the fulcrum. To achieve balance, the sum of the torques to the right of the fulcrum must equal the sum of the torques to the left of the fulcrum. This can be seen more readily here than in *Four-Foot Balance Board I* since the weights are more uniform.

Many of the objects put on the balance board do not have their mass at a single point. Their mass, and hence their weight, is spread throughout their substance. When you think about the distance of the weight from the fulcrum, you can think about the distributed weight and distance, but it's easier to think about the weight as if it were all at one point. This point is known as the *center-of-mass*. See more about the center-of-mass in the overview of *The Physics and Engineering of Structure.* One of the interesting results that you can see in these balances is that when the board and blocks are balanced, the center-of-mass of the entire system (board and blocks) is directly over the fulcrum. This is another example showing that the center-of-mass has to be over the supporting base for a structure to stand.

Extensions

◆ If students are ready for a challenge, have them try to balance a board, with whatever they want to put on it, on a pointed edge or triangular fulcrum. (You can make such a fulcrum by cutting a 4-inch-long 2-by-2 board lengthwise, on its diagonal.) They will find that this challenge is impossible to meet. No matter how carefully you try, the balance is always unstable. Even if you get it momentarily balanced, the slightest breeze or wiggle will tip it over. This type of fulcrum does not have the self-correcting property of a curved fulcrum. The system is only balanced when the center of gravity of both the board and the weights are directly over the fulcrum point. This is similar to trying to balance a stick on the end of your finger—try it without moving the hand on which it rests.

However, there is a way to solve this problem. If you attach weights rigidly (perhaps by taping them) to the bottom side of the board you can lower the center of gravity and restore the stability. The lowered center of gravity produces a balance with a self-correcting motion. It's like dangling a stick from your fingers rather than balancing it above your hand.

This extension works best in conjunction with or following the *Three-Dimensional Balance* activity.

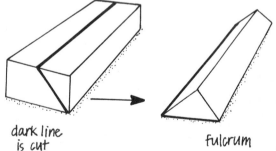

dark line
is cut

fulcrum

Little Balance Board

TIME

◆ 1 hour

PREPARATION

◆ Cut boards, make fulcrums, and gather material for weights.
◆ Set out materials.

GROUPING

◆ Two to four per group

MATERIALS

(per group)

◆ A yardstick cut in two. Use one half.
◆ One fulcrum, which can be made from a 4-inch piece of $\frac{3}{4}$-inch dowel (or $\frac{1}{2}$-inch round molding). For a nonslip fulcrum, coat half of the dowel thinly with white glue and roll it in fine sand. Tape the dowel to a wooden base.
◆ Assorted small items to balance (bottle caps, metals washers, sugar cubes, pieces of clay, and/or sand in containers)
◆ One set of about uniform weights (e.g., sugar cubes or small wooden blocks)

TEACHER TIPS

◆ This activity works well as one of several balance activities (such as *Four-Foot Balance Board I* and *II, Two-Dimensional* and *Three-Dimensional Balance*) arranged in centers around the classroom.

Context

The *Little Balance Board* activity may be used along with the *Four-Foot Balance Board* activities. Students explore the same conceptual realm with both sets of equipment. However, since student learning is often context-dependent, by changing the scale and doing many of the same things with the smaller balance, student understanding can be enhanced and broadened.

What It Is

See the *Four-Foot Balance Board* activities for ideas on activities using these materials.

Jan.26,19,

I Balanec Experiment
I balanced unifix cubes on my
Balance Experiment. I had a ruler
for the Balanc board. There was
three uxifix cubes on one
side. The other side had four.

I think why It's balanceing
is the ruler is not in the
middle of the fulcrum.

Discussing Results

See the *Four-Foot Balance Board* activities for discussion ideas.

In addition, ask students:

◆ What is the same here as with the big balance board?

◆ What is different here from the big balance board?

What's Going On

See the *Four-Foot Balance Board* activities and the overview of *The Physics and Engineering of Structure* for descriptions of the concepts of torque and center-of-mass. The major difference here is that the weights are relatively larger (compared to the curvature of the fulcrum) than with the big balance board. This creates a relatively high center-of-mass, causing the little balance board to be less stable (harder to balance) than the big balance board.

Extensions

See the *Four-Foot Balance Board* activities and other balance activities.

Two-Dimensional Balance

TIME

◆ 1 hour

PREPARATION

◆ Cut boards, make fulcrums, and gather materials for weights.
◆ Set out materials.

GROUPING

◆ Two to four per group

MATERIALS
(per group)

◆ One irregularly shaped board about 16 inches in its largest dimension cut from $\frac{1}{4}$-inch masonite or plywood (see illustration below)
◆ One spherical fulcrum (see inset instructions)
◆ Assorted weights such as large and small washers or film canisters full of sand

TEACHER TIPS

◆ This activity works well as one of several balance activities (such as *Four-Foot Balance Board I* and *II*, *Little Balance Board*, and *Three-Dimensional Balance*) done in tandem in centers around the classroom.

Context

Balance is often thought of as a one-dimensional phenomenon, as in balance along a board, a seesaw, or a pan balance. In this activity, students explore balances where they can move weights not just left and right, but also back and forth. It should be done along with other balance activities or following one-dimensional balances.

What It Is

In this activity students are asked to explore the balance of an odd-shaped, flat board sitting on a spherical fulcrum. Time should be allotted for play with the board, fulcrum, and other materials to allow the students to discover what can be done with these materials. You can encourage or extend exploration with questions like the following:

◆ Can you balance the irregularly shaped board on the spherical fulcrum?

◆ Can you make it level?

◆ Can you balance it in a tipped position?

sample board shapes

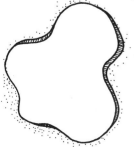

Students often raise the question, "Is it really balanced if it isn't level?" This provides a good opportunity for discussion. Often, the class decides that it wants to invent a new word or word combinations to differentiate balanced-level from balanced-askew. Ask these additional questions:

◆ Once you get it balanced, can you add weights to it?

◆ How far can you tip the shape before it falls off the fulcrum?

◆ Try variations of balancing three equal weights on the board. Can you balance them so that they are in a line? Can you balance them so that they are not in a line?

Students can play a game on a balanced shape. Add a weight, and make the shape tip. The partner adds a weight in an attempt to level the board. A variation is to scatter a bunch of weights about a shape and then balance it on a ball. Students alternately remove weights. The game is over when the board tips over.

Discussing Results

In the class discussion of observations and discoveries, it is useful to have students illustrate their statements by demonstrating them with the equipment.

You can elicit ideas by asking about specifics. For instance, "Does it matter how far away from the fulcrum you put a weight?" "If you keep the distance from the fulcrum fixed, does it matter what direction you move the weight?"

What's Going On

Torque is weight (or any force) times distance from the fulcrum. In this activity, it becomes clear that you can't just look at the distance, but you must also consider the direction. One way to think about this is to consider the distance left or right of the fulcrum and the distance forward or backward from the fulcrum for each separate weight. To achieve balance, the sum of the torque to the left and right must be equal as well as the sum of the torques forward and backward. See the overview of *The Physics and Engineering of Structure* for more on the concept of torque.

As in the board balances, when the shape and weights are balanced, the center-of-mass of the entire system (shape and weights) is directly over the fulcrum. This is another example showing that the center-of-mass has to be over the supporting base for a structure to stand.

Extensions

◆ For the uniform straight board without weights, the center-of-mass was in the middle. For these odd-shaped, cutout boards, the position of the center-of-mass is not so clear. To find the center-of-mass of the board, students can use a method described in the *Center-of-Mass* activity's third *Extension* suggestion. If this point of center-of-mass is placed directly over the fulcrum, the board will

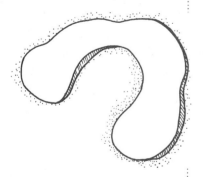

balance. It is possible to cut out a shape where the center-of-mass is not contained within the shape. It is nice to have one of these shapes in your set of boards. Ask the students, "What can you do to make this board balance?" The solution is to put additional weights on it.

◆ See other balance activities.

Making the Materials

Spherical fulcrums can be made by wedging a rubber ball or old tennis ball in a cup or juice can that has been cut to about half the height of the ball.

Center-of-Mass

TIME

◆ 30–60 minutes

PREPARATION

◆ Set out materials.

GROUPING

◆ Individuals or pairs

MATERIALS
(Per student or pair)

◆ Tinker Toy™ stand or $\frac{1}{4}$-inch dowel
◆ Scissors
◆ Different-sized weights
◆ Several squares of cardboard

Context

Center-of-mass is a term students may not know, but they are familiar with the principle through basic activities such as block building, climbing, and balancing themselves on elevated surfaces. This activity gives students an opportunity to explore center-of-mass and balance using common materials. It also connects well with the *Two-Dimensional Balance* activity.

What It Is

Working alone or in pairs, students are given cardboard squares to cut into irregular shapes (they can either create shapes or copy the silhouettes of animals or other irregular figures). Ask the students to take Tinker Toys™ and create flagpole-like stands (or if they are using dowels, have them set the dowels in cups of sand). Then ask them to see if they can balance their shapes on the top of the Tinker Toys™.

Either before they begin, or during a second attempt, ask them to predict where the center-of-mass—or balancing point—of their shape is by marking it with an *X*.

Discussing Results

Try asking the following questions:

◆ On what did you base your prediction?

◆ As you tried different shapes, how did your predictions change?

◆ Did you find any shapes that didn't have a center-of-mass? How could that be? (If the shape has a cutout center, the center-of-mass might be in the cutaway space.) Is there a way of balancing that shape? How about using two Tinker Toys™?

◆ How large a shape can you balance on a Tinker Toy™? Why is it more difficult?

◆ Could you change a large shape to make it easier to balance? (Hang from a string attached to the center-of-mass, bend corners down, etc.)

What's Going On

The center-of-mass of a flat object is the point where it balances. It's as if all of the mass, and hence weight, of that object were concentrated at that point.

See the overview of *The Physics and Engineering of Structure* for more information.

Extensions

◆ Paint shapes and hang them from their center-of-mass as a mobile.

◆ Explore further by hanging or setting small weights on top of cardboard.

◆ You can also find the center-of-mass of your cardboard shape as follows: Put three small holes at various points near the edge of your shape. Using one of the holes, hang your shape on a nail or pin. Put a weight (e.g., a heavy washer) on a string and hang the string from the nail. The string creates a vertical line, called a *plumb line*. Draw a line on the cardboard shape along the string. Hang the cardboard from a different hole and trace the line again. The lines should cross at the center-of-mass of the board. To check, hang from the third hole. The string should pass over where the two lines cross. This method also works well for finding the center-of-mass for the odd-shaped boards used in the *Two-Dimensional Balance* activity.

Three-Dimensional Balance

TIME

◆ 1 hour

PREPARATION

◆ Make pointed fulcrums and stands.
◆ Set out materials.

GROUPING

◆ Individuals or pairs

MATERIALS
(per pair)

◆ One stand (see *Making the Materials* inset at the end of this activity)
◆ One pointed fulcrum (see *Making the Materials* inset)
◆ One Tinker Toys™ construction-sized set (can be shared by four students)

TEACHER TIPS

◆ We prefer the old wooden Tinker Toys™ (for aesthetic reasons). However, they can now only be found in specialty catalogues and at garage sales. The new plastic Tinker Toys™ do work for this activity, but you may have to jam some paper or clay in the plastic holes to help hold the dowel fulcrum in place.

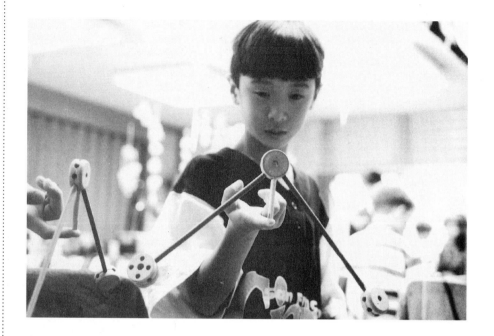

Context

This activity gives experience with three-dimensional balance. It is especially good for getting a feel for the concept of center-of-mass. In this activity, students explore balances where they can move weights not just left and right, up and down, or back and forth, but in all three dimensions. It should be done along with other balance activities or following one-dimensional balances.

What It Is

Put the pointed fulcrum into one of the Tinker Toy™ connectors, with the pointed side out. Challenge the students to add Tinker Toy™ pieces in such a way that the point sits on the end of the stand and balances. Suggest that they get a feel for it by trying it on a finger. Give students some time to struggle with the challenge on their own. If they need help, suggest trying some systematic alternatives. For example, try all long sticks or all short sticks; try sticks going up or sticks going down.

Once they get it balanced, have them experiment with different arrangements. What additions or changes make it more stable? What makes it less stable? Try making it more or less symmetrical. Try to make it taller. How does adding or

moving pieces affect the way it moves and sways? Once the basic balance problem is solved, this becomes a design question. Students can build something that looks like a figure. They may want to add decorations. See *Extensions* below.

Discussing Results

In the class discussion of observations and discoveries, students should share one of their balanced constructions. Having students describe their process of solving the problem is very useful here. Questions you might ask include, "Can you remove any of the pieces and still have a balance?" The key observation to elicit from the students is that the lower the weight (below the fulcrum), the better the balance.

What's Going On

In this activity, if the center-of-mass (see the overview of *The Physics and Engineering of Structure*) is below the fulcrum, then the construction will balance. The farther it is below the fulcrum, the more stable it is. If the center-of-mass is above the fulcrum, the object will tip over and fall. In addition, the construction must be bal-

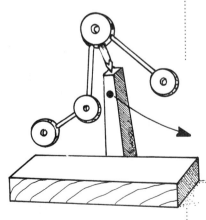

center of mass of
"tinker toy system" is
below the balance point

anced horizontally in the other two dimensions, left and right and back and forth. If it is not balanced this way, it will tip over. If the center-of-mass is low enough, it can tip until it self-corrects and balances out horizontally. The simplest solution to the problem is to add two long rods diagonally downward from the connector on either side of the fulcrum with connectors as weights on the ends.

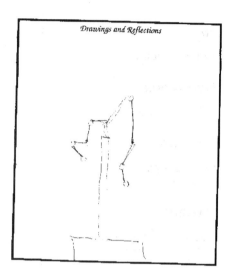

Observations:	Questions:
Tinker Toy 3 strategies Build down Build out and use lots of wieght I thought it was hard.	If you Build up would it work

Drawings and Reflections

This kind of balance is known as a *stabile* (as opposed to a *mobile*). When swinging, the balance acts as a compound pendulum. The swinging in the larger pieces can be quite slow and elegant.

Extensions

◆ The simplest extension is to have students build stabiles, a counterpart to mobiles. Stabiles use the balance principles explored in this activity to create kinetic works of art. Use your imagination to turn any variety of materials into stabiles. The key elements are a stand to balance on, a fulcrum or pivot point, and a distribution of weight to create a stable balance. There are many toys and folk-art pieces that use this balance principle.

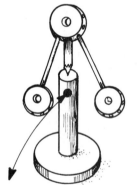

center of mass of "tinker toy system"
is below the balance point

Making the Materials

Stands—You can use a 12-inch to 24-inch 1-by-2 nailed to a scrap 2-by-4 or larger base. Another simple stand is a $\frac{3}{4}$-inch dowel or a piece of 1-by-2 in a coffee can full of sand.

Fulcrums—Fulcrums can be made by sharpening the end of a $\frac{1}{4}$-inch dowel with a pencil sharpener and cutting it off at about the $1\frac{1}{2}$-inch mark.

Body Balance

TIME

◆ 20–30 minutes

PREPARATION

◆ Clear floor space.

GROUPING

◆ Pairs (one performer/one observer)

MATERIALS

◆ Optional: 6-foot length of string, large mirror

Context

Our first and most basic understanding of balance, stability, torques, and center-of-mass comes from our physical experiences of these phenomena in our own bodies. For students with strong kinesthetic learning styles, the body is still a primary mode for learning about these concepts. This activity complements many of the balance activities. By changing the scale and using their own bodies as the weights, students are given an opportunity to see the same phenomena in a new context, thus broadening their conceptual understanding.

In addition, body balance and stability play an important role in athletics and dance. This provides an important avenue for bringing in students' experiences and broadening their classroom work.

Body Balance

What It Is

Ask your students: "In what ways can you or can't you move your own body without falling over?" If you have dealt with center-of-mass in previous activities, than begin this activity by talking about the body's center-of-mass. You can illustrate that the human body's center-of-mass lies somewhere near the navel; if we bend too far to the right or left, or too far forward or backward, without compensating with a counterbalance, our bodies will fall over. This is another example of the fact that a structure's center-of-mass must be directly over its base for the structure to stand.

Body Movements

Have the performer from each pair of students stand up and try to make one simple motion of his/her body without moving the rest. For instance, suggest that the performer bend at the waist while keeping every other muscle perfectly still. Tell the observer to note carefully what happens to the performer's center-of-mass. Does the observer note any compensations or adjustments the performer makes while bending?

Experiment with small movements (fingers) as well as large ones (arms and legs), moving limbs in front of the body and behind. After a while, ask the students to change roles, so that each has the opportunity to observe what happens.

(If you do this activity with individuals, tape a string down the center of a mirror. The student can observe how his/her body moves in relation to the string.)

A nice activity to end this session involves asking a student to bend over at the waist to pick up an object (e.g., a soft-drink bottle) on the ground. Then move the bottle closer to the wall and have the student stand with his/her heels and back against the wall and bend over and pick up the object again. The wall interferes with students' ability to move their bottom back to compensate for the weight going forward. When they are against the wall it becomes impossible to bend over.

Hand-to-Hand Wrestling

Next, form groups of four out of two sets of pairs. It is important to establish the rules of this activity before you explain what it is. The most important rule is that there's no grabbing or pulling. Ask the question, "How can you push somebody off balance?" One set of partners stand facing each other, placing their palms against each other's. The other set of partners sits off to the side to act as referees. When the referees say "Go!" the standing partners try to push each other off balance *without grabbing or pulling* or moving their feet. The "game" is over when one partner moves a foot. Then the pairs switch roles: the referees become the wrestlers, and the wrestlers the referees.

Discussing Results

Ask the students the following questions:

Body Movements

◆ What did the observers notice? What did the performers feel?

◆ Did the performers' bodies adjust or compensate for the physical movements? How?

Body Balance

◆ Could the performers prevent their bodies from adjusting? How?

Look at the idea of physical compensation for outside forces in the outside world.

◆ When you walk, does your body tilt or react to your legs moving?

◆ Do animals adjust their bodies when they move? Ask for examples.

◆ Do other structures adjust when the center-of-mass shifts? What about bridges in the wind? Skyscrapers in earthquakes? TV antennae in rainstorms? Palm trees in hurricanes?

Hand-to-Hand Wrestling

◆ What was the best strategy to push your partner off balance?

◆ Did your strategy change in the middle of the game? Why or why not?

◆ How could you keep your balance?

What's Going On

The key idea in this activity is that when the center-of-mass moves outside the area directly over the base, the structure topples. The center-of-mass of the human body standing straight is near the belly button. When the body tilts, it compensates with a counterbalance. For instance, when you hold your arms out forward, the rest of your body tilts slightly backward. When you bend at the waist, you move your bottom backward to compensate. In this case, your center-of-mass may be out of your body just in front of your navel. It is, however, still directly over the base of your feet, providing balance. Fortunately, the body has an innate sense of maintaining balance that allows us to stand upright, lest we tumble with each movement. Animals with four legs have a wider base and therefore are more stable. Their bodies also adjust with movement to maintain stability and balance.

In the hand-to-hand wrestling activity, performers had to compensate for horizontal forces (their opponents' pushes) as well as their own weight. Here, a broad base (feet spread apart) and low center-of-mass were helpful. With one leg held back, a force countering the opponent's push could be exerted.

Extensions

◆ Try adding weights (books will do) to the outstretched hands of a balanced person.

◆ Try balancing on one foot.

◆ In many sports and in dance, balance and awareness of the body's "center" is very important. In football, runners with a low center-of-mass are harder to bring down. The low center-of-mass and wide stance makes them much more stable. Analyzing photos of athletes and dancers for their balance is a nice way to get students to think about the concepts of center-of-mass, balance, and stability.

Planks on Scales

TIME

- 30 minutes for group activity
- 15–30 minutes for individual exploration

PREPARATION

- Set up a demonstration at the front of the class.

GROUPING

- Whole group, then individual exploration

MATERIALS

- Two bathroom scales
- One 6-foot 2-by-4 plank (or wider; e.g., 2-by-6 or 2-by-8)
- Two or four shorter 2-by-4s to raise/support the plank on the scales

Context

There are innumerable examples where weight is supported from a few or several points. Our own weight is supported by our feet. Houses and decks are supported on posts and cement footings. Bridges are supported by points at either end. Buildings are supported by concrete pads. Even when two people carry a box, the weight is supported by both people. In many of the building activities in this book, structures support weight at feet touching the ground or at various joints. How is this weight distributed? How much weight is supported by each point? These questions are explored here.

This activity gives the students an opportunity to experiment with the phenomena concerning how weight is distributed over a surface and supported by points on the base. It is most effective when it follows balance and center-of-mass activities.

What It Is

Place a scale on the floor and adjust the balance to zero. Ask a student to stand on the scale and read his/her weight. Write this down on the board or chart paper. Place another scale just next to the first and adjust the balance to zero. Ask the students to predict what will happen to the scale readings when the student places one foot on one scale and the other foot on the other scale. Ask the student to put one foot on each scale and to stand in the middle, perfectly still. Record the results on the board. (The weight ought to be divided evenly between the two scales and should be equal to the original weight recorded on one scale.)

Separate the scales and place the ends of the 6-foot plank on each of the scales. *Be sure to put the plank on the scales so that it can't slip off.* Readjust the scales so that they balance to zero. Have the same student stand in the middle of the plank. Ask the class to guess what the scales read, and record the measurements. Have the student move closer to one of the scales, perhaps three quarters along the plank. Again predict and record the readings. You can have the student move backward and forward and watch and record how the measurements change. You can also have him/her stand still, with feet wide apart, and shift his/her weight by leaning into one or the other of their legs.

Raise one of the scales on the shorter 2-by-4s so that the large plank slopes downward. Predict the reading on each scale if the student stands in the center. Look at what happens if the student stands perpendicular to the board (the downhill scale should have a higher reading) versus perpendicular to the floor (both scales should read about the same). Have the student move from one side to the other, recording the reading on each scale at various points.

Discussing Results

Ask the students what has happened and why. Extrapolate from your findings and ask the students how the same principle of distributing weight might be used in constructing a building or a bridge or one of their own constructions. For instance, how does the weight supported by piers on either side of a bridge change as a heavy truck rolls across? Also, the walls of a house support the house's second story. Discuss how placement of furniture, bathroom fixtures, and other weights in the second story affect the force distribution on the supporting walls.

What's Going On

The reading on a scale shows how hard its internal spring pushes up to balance the weight pushing down on it. If you stand on two scales, only half of your weight is pushing down on each scale, so each of the scales only has to "push up" half as hard as before. The total upward push of the two scales equals the total downward pull of your body (in other words, your weight). (See the overview of *The Physics and Engineering of Structure* for more on this subject.)

When you stand on two scales, the reading on each of the scales depends on how much of your weight is being "pulled down" into each of your legs (and consequently, how much each of the scales has to push up to counterbalance the downward force). It is easy to shift your weight from foot to foot and change the reading on each scale. However, the sum of the two scale readings will always be equal to your weight.

When you stand on a plank placed between the two scales, the same principle applies. The total weight on the scales is the sum of your weight and the weight of the plank; the total force upward balances the total force downward. But there is an additional physical principle which you can observe using a plank: the effects of *torques*.

You can observe that the reading on a scale depends on how close you are standing to it. As you move along the plank, the readings increase or decrease depending on whether you are nearing or leaving the scale. This weight distribution is a result of the balance of torques (see the overview of *The Physics and Engineering of Structure*).

Torque is force times distance from a pivot point. In this activity, force = weight; distance = distance from your body to a scale. To balance the torques, the force (weight) on one scale times your distance from that scale must be equal to the force (weight) on the other scale times your distance from that scale. Suppose you weigh 120 pounds and are standing 2 feet to the right of one scale and 4 feet to the left of another. You can predict that the scale on the left will read 80 pounds and the scale on the right will read 40 pounds. To balance the torques, the force times the distance for each scale must be equal. In this case, 2 feet × 80 pounds = 4 feet × 40 pounds.

Extension

Real Life

Look at examples from everyday life where weight is supported by two or more points. These could range from people carrying something to bridges and buildings sitting on concrete footings.

Torque Activity

To point out the effect of weight at a distance from a pivot point, hang a heavy backpack or purse on an outstretched arm. Try hanging it near the shoulder and then near the hand. The object feels much heavier near the hand. Since the weight of the object has not changed, the difference that is felt is a change in the torque—the force (weight) times the distance (in this case, the distance from the shoulder). In this example, as you move the weight of the bag farther from your shoulder, the increasing torque will tend to twist your arm about your shoulder.

PART TWO

The Mathematics of Scale

Note to the Teacher

The following conceptual overview is for you. Its purpose is to provide you with a conceptual framework for organizing your teaching and responding to student discoveries. For your students, developing an understanding of these ideas will grow out of experiencing the phenomena that are inherent in the activities.

You should not feel that you have to understand all of this information before you start teaching. Try these activities along with your students, using this conceptual overview as your own reference. Engaging in the activities will clarify many of the concepts for you as well as for your students.

Context

When we look at structures on different scales, both physical and biological, we notice major differences and some similarities. Since many physical elements of structure (such as weight and strength) depend on different dimensions, many of these structural differences can be explained purely in terms of scale change. The next section includes activities that deal with proportion and with linear, area, and volume dimensions. The activities explore these concepts and how the relationship between them changes with changes in scale. In order to understand the effects of scale on structure, it is important to have a grounding in these essentially mathematical arenas.

Concepts

When we talk about dimension, we are talking about length, area, and volume. Think of length not just as a straight line, but as any linear dimension, including perimeters, diameters, and circumferences. Area is not just length times width, but the covering of any surface, flat, curved, or irregular, or the covering of an imagined cross-section. Volume is the amount of space an object occupies. Several of the activities in this section are designed to help broaden student understanding of lengths, areas, and volumes.

An easy way to look at changes in scale is to observe what happens as you "grow" a cube (see the *Growing Cubes* activity). If you can understand how a cube grows, then you can understand the scale relationships for any object of any regular or irregular shape, since all shapes grow according to the same geometric rules.

For this example, imagine you are building with one-centimeter unit cubes. (Each unit cube is 1 cm wide, 1 cm tall, and 1 cm deep.) The area of the base of this cube is one square centimeter (1 cm²). Since a cube has six sides, the total surface area of the unit cube is 6 cm². The volume of this unit cube is one cubic centimeter (1 cm³).

The chart shows the growth of area and volume of the cube as the linear dimension is doubled, tripled, quadrupled, etc.

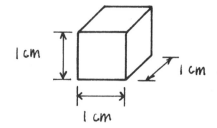

1 cm
1 cm
1 cm

Length of Edge (cm)	Area of Base (cm²)	Area of Total Surface (cm²)	Volume (cm³)
1	1	6	1
2	4	24	8
3	9	54	27
4	16	96	64
5	25	150	125
6	36	216	216
7	49	294	343
8	64	384	512
9	81	486	729
10	100	600	1000
. . .	. . .	. . .	. . .

As the length of the side increases, all linear dimensions increase. If you triple the length, the perimeter triples and the diagonals triple. Area grows faster. If you triple the length, the area goes up by a factor of 9. Volume grows fastest of all: if you triple the length, the volume increases by a factor of 27. If you like equations, you can think of this relationship as n = length, n^2 : area, and n : volume (where the symbol : means "is proportional to"). Look at the numbers on the cube chart. If the left-hand column (length of side) is n, then you'll find that the next column (area of base) is n squared (n^2). The column listing volume is n cubed (n^3).

As you move up and down in scale, the length, area, and volume change at very different rates. This is not only true for cubes—as long as the proportions of the object are unchanged as it grows, these growth rules are true for any shape, as illustrated in the *Cylinders and Scale* and the *Cones and Scale* activities.

Area Activities

TIME

◆ 45 minutes

PREPARATION

◆ Set out materials.

GROUPING

◆ Individuals or pairs

MATERIALS
(per student or pair)

◆ Several sheets of centimeter graph paper
◆ Construction paper cut into about a dozen 3-cm-by-3-cm squares

TEACHER TIPS

◆ For younger students, you may want to use graph paper with larger squares.

Context

Looking at changes in areas and volumes as you change scale is key to understanding what happens to structures at different scales. In order to understand these changes students must develop a broad understanding of area and volume.

Area is more than just length times width. It is an amount of surface. Students sometimes talk about the measure of area as the amount of little squares that it takes to cover something.

Volume is not just liquid measurements like gallons or cubic centimeters, nor is it simply length times width times height. Volume is the amount of space taken up or enclosed by something.

There are a number of good math materials around that introduce students to the concepts of area and volume in very concrete ways. See *Read More About It* at the end of this activity.) We are not trying to substitute for them. The simple activities

Area Activities

presented here can help students develop an understanding of the concept of area, and consequently of physical scaling.

Students without much experience with area will benefit from working with a number of materials of the type cited above before plunging into the activities of this section. For those with a good background, this activity serves as a nice reminder of the breadth of the concept of area.

What It Is

Foot Area

Have each student predict how much surface their foot will cover. To discover the accuracy of their predictions, they can trace their foot on a piece of centimeter graph paper and count the number of squares within the foot's outline. To keep track of the count, write successive numbers in each square within the outline of the foot. Talk about combining partial squares to create whole squares to be used in the count.

Sequence the papers to show the smallest to largest foot outlines. Compare the sequence results to the heights of the students. Is the student with the biggest foot also the tallest?

Centimeter Art

Discuss the various ways you can divide a square centimeter on the graph paper into halves. Hand out the graph paper, one or more sheets to each student. Have the students create a design (they could do their name, or draw an animal, or a house, etc.), using whole or half centimeters. Have them color in the design. After they have finished, have them count the centimeters that have been colored in, adding up the halves. Have them write the total number of square centimeters at the bottom of the design.

Area Estimates

In this activity students use the 3-cm-by-3-cm squares of construction paper as area units. Have the students select a flat object (a book, a desk, a hand) and ask them to estimate how many construction paper squares will be needed to cover the object. Have them completely cover the object with squares, cutting the squares into fractions where needed to cover corners or irregular edges, etc. Count the total number of squares (adding up the fractions of squares) and write it down next to the original estimate. Then have the students select more objects and continue guessing, keeping a record of how far off their guesses are from the actual number.

Discussing Results

Students should talk about their techniques for determining area. Were they surprised at the number of squares that their feet covered? How about other objects?

Because irregular objects cannot be exactly covered by complete squares, parts of squares have to be combined to get final results. Students are often concerned that they did not get exact results. Discuss approximations and how they work in real life, and look at how close their approximations were to the exact numbers.

This work can lead to a discussion of where in the world area measurements are necessary. Examples include measurements for rugs, linoleum or floor tiles; countertop tiles, lawn area or garden plots; and areas of walls for painting.

What's Going On

Area is not just length times width. It has to do with what it takes to cover something or the amount of surface something covers. This activity helps to develop or reinforce an intuition for this concept of area.

Extensions

Body Area Estimates

Following the same procedure as in *Area Estimates* above, estimate and discover the surface area of people's body parts (we suggest arms, legs, and heads). Using one live model (as opposed to several students) also tends to keep things under control.

Quilt Design

Cut different-colored construction paper into 3-cm squares. Experiment with patterns while making "quilts" by gluing the construction paper squares onto 30-cm-by-30-cm sheets of graph paper. Construction paper squares may be cut in half for aesthetic effects.

Use of Area Measure

Have students find examples of where area measure is used outside the school. For example, paint covers a certain number of square feet and so painters need to know surface area. Carpets are sold in square yards. Roofing material is sold by the "square." A square of shingles covers 100 square feet. Land area is measured in acres. One acre is 43,560 square feet.

Read More About It

The following materials are excellent sources of activities that help students learn more about geometry and especially about the concepts of area and volume.

Marilyn Burns, *A Collection of Math Lessons: Grades 1 to 3,* Reading, Mass.: Addison-Wesley, 1992.

Marilyn Burns, *A Collection of Math Lessons: Grades 3 to 6,* Reading, Mass.: Addison-Wesley, 1987.

Marilyn Burns, *A Collection of Math Lessons: Grades 6 to 8,* Reading, Mass.: Addison-Wesley, 1990.

Marilyn Burns, *About Teaching Mathematics: A K–8 Resource,* Reading, Mass.: Addison-Wesley, 1992.

Marilyn Burns, *The Goodtime Math Event Book,* Mountain View, Calif.: Creative Publications, 1977.

Area Activities

EQUALS, *Get It Together: Math Problems for Groups: Grades 4–12,* Berkeley, Calif.: Lawrence Hall of Science, 1989.

Judy Goodnow, Shirley Hoogeboom, and Ann Roper, *Moving on with Tangrams: Intermediate Problem Solving Activities,* Mountain View, Calif.: Creative Publications, 1988.

Beyond Activities Project, *Polyhedraville: An Expansion of 3-Dimensional Geometry,* Chico, Calif.: Department of Mathematics and Statistics, California State University at Chico, 1991.

Introduction to Cubes

TIME

◆ 30–60 minutes

PREPARATION

◆ Set out sugar cubes and graph paper on the tables.

GROUPING

◆ Individuals or pairs

MATERIALS
(per student or pair)

◆ 64–100 sugar cubes (sugar cubes are the cheapest way we have found of getting a large number of uniform cubes)
◆ Paper

TEACHER TIPS

◆ Warn students about eating dirty sugar cubes. To head off this problem, some teachers give each student one clean cube to eat before building.
◆ Cleanup is simplified if students work with their sugar cubes on paper. The loose sugar granules can then be easily emptied into the wastebasket.

Context

Cubes are very useful for exploring and examining relative growth of lengths, areas, and volumes as you scale up, as they are easy to measure and the numbers come out exactly. Before getting into more focused work with cubes, students need the opportunity to do some free building with cubes. You can use the results of this free building to have students generate their own operational definitions of area, volume, and linear measures that will be useful in further activities. For instance, length could be the number of sugar cube edges that would fit along the line being measured.

What It Is

Start by asking students to build with their sugar cubes for about fifteen minutes. Students build a variety of structures. Some may be figurative, looking like houses or walls. Others will be abstract, like big cubes or pyramids. At the end of the time period, have your students save their structures and tell them you now want them to take measurements of length, surface area, and volume for their structure.

It is useful to establish units of convenience for working with these cubes in this activity. You and your class can invent your own names for these units based on the dimensions of the sugar cube. We came up with units as follows:

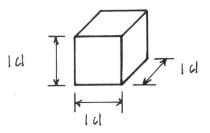

Length—The natural unit of length is the length of the edge of the sugar cube. We call this unit the *cube length* or *cl*. The perimeter of a single sugar cube is 4 cl's.

Area—The natural unit of area is the surface covered by one face of the sugar cube. We call this unit the *face*. The total surface area of a single sugar cube is 6 faces.

Volume—The natural unit of volume is the space occupied by one sugar cube. We call this unit the *sugar cube*, or *sc*. A 2-by-2-by-2 cube has a volume of 8 sc's.

Discussing Results

Ask students to determine some lengths on their structure. An easy one to start with is height: "How tall is your structure?" For some structures, length and width are also natural dimensions to determine. Here's a harder one: Ask students to determine the perimeter of the base of their structure. This raises lots of questions. What if someone built a "fence" enclosing a space—do you count just outside perimeter or inside too? How about if the fence has a doorway? These lead to interesting questions about what perimeter is, and allows the class to come up with definitions for different kinds of perimeter. When this discussion is complete, have students record the perimeters of their structures on chart paper for comparison. Have students look at the structures with particularly small perimeters. What do they look like? In what ways are they similar? Have them look at structures with particularly large perimeters. What do they look like? In what ways are they similar? What are the differences and similarities between structures with small perimeters and structures with large perimeters?

Ask students to determine some areas on their structure. A good starting point is area of the base (i.e., the area that it sits on). Even this raises some questions. For fencelike structures, do you count the area enclosed? If there are gaps between cubes should the area in them be counted? The simplest way to go is to count the number of cube faces touching the ground. Your group may want to go with several options, each having a different name. For instance, in fencelike structures they may want to define an area enclosed. Another possible area to measure is the total surface area. This is basically the number of faces that are not touching other cubes. You could also talk about it as the number of faces that are exposed. After this discussion, have students record the areas of their structures on chart paper for comparison. Have students look at the structures with particularly small areas. What do they look like? In what ways are they similar? Have them look at structures with particularly large areas. What do they look like? In what ways are they similar? What are the differences and similarities between structures with small areas and structures with large areas?

Finally, ask students to determine the volume of their structure. For solid structures this is relatively easy: it is the number of sugar cubes used to construct it. However, some structures raise questions. If a structure is cuplike, do you count the volume that the "cup" would hold? Also, for structures with gaps between sugar cubes, the structure takes up more space than if the cubes were tightly packed. How do you count volume on those?

What's Going On

In looking at lengths, areas, and volumes of these structures, a number of questions arise around how you want to define these quantities. The discussion around these questions is extremely valuable. It helps to stretch your students' thinking about just what these quantities are and prepares them for further activities.

Extensions

◆ You may want to do a great deal more building with sugar cubes, as they are a flexible building material. They can be sanded with fine sandpaper to make wedge-shaped blocks for arches or for making blocks with fractional widths. They can be cemented together with white glue or frosting. Any further building provides more opportunities to look at lengths, areas, and volumes.

Growing Cubes

Time

◆ 30–60 minutes

Preparation

◆ Prepare blank cube charts (see below).
◆ Set out sugar cubes and paper on the tables.

Grouping

◆ Pairs or groups of four

Materials
(per student or pair)

◆ 64 sugar cubes
◆ One blank cube growth chart (from Appendix C)
◆ Paper

Teacher Tips

◆ Warn students about eating dirty sugar cubes. To head off this problem, some teachers give each student one clean cube to eat before building.
◆ Cleanup is simplified if students work with their sugar cubes on paper. The loose sugar granules can then be easily emptied into the wastebasket.

Context

A key to understanding the way in which scale affects structure is understanding the differences in the change of lengths, area, and volume as you scale up. The two central ideas here are that as you scale up proportionally (i.e., keep things the same shape but change the size) (1) area grows faster than length and volume grows faster than area and (2) all lengths grow at the same rate and all areas grow at the same rate on a scaled object.

Work with cubes is an essential beginning to understanding relative growth of lengths, areas, and volumes as you scale up, since cubes are easy to measure and the numbers come out exactly right. This allows students to see the patterns of change in length, in area, and in volume without the complication of approximation and experimental error. The *Introduction to Cubes* activity should precede this activity.

What It Is

One interesting way to begin the activity is to do a small demonstration. At the front of the class, set one sugar cube on the table. Discuss the various aspects of the cube. How is it different from a square? Then ask the students, "How do you double the size of the cube?" Typically, they will answer that you should put one more sugar cube on top of the existing sugar cube, or alongside and adjacent to it. When you do this, they will see that they haven't doubled the size of the cube; instead, they have made a rectangular prism.

Try rephrasing the question as, "How do you build the next biggest cube?" You must add seven sugar cubes, for a total of eight sugar cubes, to do this. To make the next biggest cube you must double the length, double the width, and double the height. This opens up the discussion to the properties of a cube, including what surface area and volume are (see below).

It is useful to establish units in this activity. You and your class can invent your own units of convenience or use the units we define below.

Length—The natural unit of length is the length of the edge of the sugar cube. We called this unit the *cube length* or *cl.* The perimeter of a single sugar cube is 4 cl's.

Area—The natural unit of area is the surface covered by one face of the sugar cube. We call this unit the *face.* The total surface area of a single sugar cube is 6 faces.

Volume—The natural unit of volume is the space occupied by one sugar cube. We call this unit the *sugar cube,* or *sc.* A 2-by-2-by-2 cube has a volume of 8 sc's.

Each student group should start with a blank version of the chart illustrated below (see Appendix C). Discuss the measures that they will be recording on the chart. For instance, make sure everyone knows what the base is (the part of the cubes that sits on the table).

CUBE GROWTH CHART

Length of Edge (cube length)	Perimeter of Base (cube length)	Area of Base (face)	Area of Total Surface (face)	Volume (sugar cube)
1	4	1	6	1
2	8	4	24	8
3	12	9	54	27
4	16	16	96	64
5	20	25	150	125
6	24	36	216	216
7	28	49	294	343
8	32	64	384	512
9	36	81	486	729
10	40	100	600	1000
. . .	. . .	. . .	. . .	. . .

Have the students begin to construct increasingly larger cubes with their sugar cubes. Ask them to construct cubes with edge lengths of 1, 2, 3, 4, and 5 cl's or maybe more. (Look out for groups that start to build squares instead of cubes. Make sure they understand that size increases in all three dimensions.) For each cube they build, they should record lengths, areas, and volume on their chart. They may need some instruction or assistance with this on their first few cubes. To build the larger cubes, students will have to combine supplies from several groups.

Discussing Results

When the activity is finished, complete a class chart for everyone to see during the discussion. Discuss how length, area, and volume grow differently. One teacher had her students begin the discussion in class and then take their charts home over two nights for analysis. Back in class, the students discussed their findings and ideas in small groups and added to the class chart. After several days of thinking, they had a large-group discussion to share all of their ideas. To promote discussion, the following questions may be of use:

◆ What do you notice about your measurements?

◆ What patterns do you notice in the chart?

◆ What do you think is going on?

◆ Where do you think these patterns come from?

The difference in growth rate of areas and volumes is the key to understanding how scale affects structure. (This growth rate is often referred to as a change of surface-to-volume ratio with scale.) Ask the students how many sugar cubes each face of the base must support as the cube size increases.

What's Going On

As the length of the side increases, all linear dimensions increase. As you can see from the chart, if you double the side length, the perimeter of the base also doubles. If you increase the side length by a factor of 5 the perimeter is also 5 times as long. This is true for other linear dimensions as well—for instance, the length of a diagonal.

Area grows faster. In the chart you can see that if the side length doubles (from 1 to 2), the area goes up by a factor of 4. This is true of all areas: area of the base, total surface area, and area of a cross-section. If you increase the side length by a factor of 5, the area becomes 25 times as large. In general, if you make the sides of the cube n times as big, than the areas are $n \times n$ or n^2 times as big.

And volume grows fastest of all. In the chart you can see that if the side length doubles, the volume increases by a factor of 8. If you increase the side length by a factor of 5, the volume is 125 times as large. In general, if you make the sides of the cube n times as big, than the volume is $n \times n \times n$ or n^3 times as big.

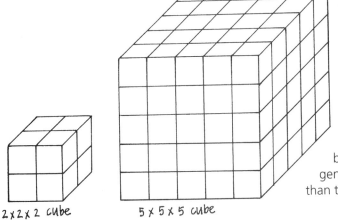

2 x 2 x 2 cube   5 x 5 x 5 cube

The key idea here is as follows:

As you move up or down in scale, length, area, and volume change at very different rates.

Very large things have a small surface area for their volume or, more formally, a low surface-to-volume ratio. This has a number of physical consequences. For instance, large trees need a lot of water to sustain their volume. Water enters the tree through the surface of the root. To increase surface area, trees have multiple branching root systems with lots of tiny root hairs instead of one big thick root. (For more examples see the *Beyond This Book* section.)

Extensions

◆ Start with some plasticene (modeling clay) cubes about the same size as sugar cubes. Ask the students how big they think the edge of a new cube will be if you combine two of the same-size plasticene cubes. If the cubes are exact duplicates, the edge of the new cube should be about 1.25 times the edge of each of the smaller cubes (the double-volume cube would have edges that are the cube root of 2 times the length of the original sides). This extension illuminates the difference between doubling the volume of the cube, which is done here, and doubling the linear dimensions. To double the length, width, and height would take seven additional cubes, not just one more.

◆ Make a plasticene sphere from 2 ounces of clay. Ask the students how much clay they think it would take to double the circumference of the sphere? to double the diameter? Since these are both linear dimensions, the amount needed to double the diameter or circumference is the same. Doubling the linear dimensions and keeping the shape the same is like doubling the length, width, and height of a cube. It would take 8 times the volume or 8 times as much clay. In this case that would be 1 pound of clay.

◆ Ask students how much bigger they think the sphere would be with twice as much clay. This is analogous to the first extension, which combines two cubes. In this case the diameter and circumference would be about 1.25 times as big.

Shrinking Cubes

TIME

◆ 30–60 minutes

PREPARATION

◆ Prepare blank charts (see below).
◆ Set out materials.

GROUPING

◆ Pairs

MATERIALS
(per pair)

◆ 8 oz. or more of plasticene (modeling clay)
◆ Small (3-inch-by-5-inch or slightly larger) block of wood, plywood, or particle board for shaping cubes
◆ Butter knife, steel rule, wire, or dental floss for cutting clay
◆ Graph paper (1 or 2 sheets)
◆ One blank cube shrinking chart (from Appendix C)
◆ Paper to work on

TEACHER TIPS

◆ Plasticene is an oil-based clay. It leaves an oily residue on surfaces. Work on paper and/or be prepared to clean desks with soap or other grease remover.

Context

This activity should be done after *Growing Cubes*. Logically, when you understand the pattern of relative growth of lengths, areas, and volumes as you scale up, you should be able to understand the patterns for scaling down. However, students need to work explicitly with lengths, areas, and volumes as object sizes diminish to understand these patterns. This activity expands their realm of thinking from large scales to small.

The two central ideas here are that as you scale down proportionally (i.e., keep things the same shape but change the size) (1) area shrinks faster than length and volume shrinks faster than area and (2) all lengths and all areas shrink at the same rate on a scaled object.

Work with cubes is an essential beginning to understanding the relative growth of lengths, areas, and volumes as you scale down because cubes are easy to work with and the results are easy to see compared to other shapes.

What It Is

This is an activity that you will probably want to take students through step by step. Begin the discussion by saying, "We have looked at the lengths, areas, and volumes of cubes and seen the pattern as we doubled, tripled, and quadrupled the sizes of the cubes. What do you think will happen if we make smaller cubes? What if we make one-half-, one-third- and one-quarter-sized cubes? Do you expect a pattern again? If so, what do you think it might be?" The answer is fractions (see chart below).

Have the students begin by making a cube out of their of clay. Although 8 ounces can be used for this activity, larger amounts of clay work even better. With 8 ounces, the one-quarter-sized linear-dimension cubes are only an eighth of an ounce of clay and hard to work with. Use the wooden block to push or pound the clay, turning it on various sides until it becomes a pretty good cube. Acknowledge to your students that the cubes constructed here will not be perfect. However, the better the cube, the easier it will be to figure out the patterns of shrinkage.

After the students make their big cube, have them outline the base on some paper. Graph paper works well, as it helps students compare areas after cutting smaller cubes.

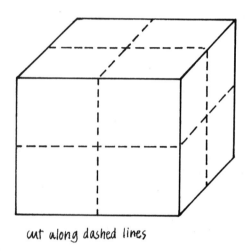

cut along dashed lines

Tell the students that you want them to cut their cube up to make a bunch of cubes half as tall, half as long, and half as wide—in other words, cubes whose edges are half as long as a big cube. Have them predict how many one-eighth-sized cubes they will get. Ask, What are the fewest number of cuts needed to get all of the little cubes? You can divide up the big cube to get eight one-half-sized cubes by making three cuts (see illustration).

After students have made the cuts, have them look at the little cubes. Each student group should start with a blank version of the chart shown below. Have students record the answers to the following questions on their charts:

◆ What is the edge length of the one-half-sized cubes compared to the big cube? (One-half of the big cube's edge length.)

◆ What is the area of the base and total surface area compared to the big cube? (One-fourth of the corresponding big-cube areas.)

◆ What is the volume compared to the big cube? Since all of the little cubes are identical, each of their volumes is just the volume of the big cube divided by the total number of little cubes. (For example, if you have eight little cubes, each has a volume of one-eighth of the big cube.)

◆ How many little cubes did you get?

Have students use the outline of the big cube base to help answer the following question:

◆ What is the total surface area of all the little cubes compared to the big cube?

Following the first set of cuts, have students discuss their process and results. Was it hard or easy to cut little cubes? How about making them even? What techniques worked well for getting even cubes? Often measuring and drawing lines on the big cube will help with the cutting. How did the students go about making their measurements? One way of figuring the area of the base is to see how many bases of the small cubes fit in the outline of the big cube.

After this discussion have students rebuild their big cube. Then have them cut smaller cubes to see the pattern emerge. It is usually necessary to do at least two more sets of cuts; one where the big cube is cut into little cubes whose lengths are one-third that of the big cube, and one where the big cube is cut into little cubes whose lengths are one-fourth that of the big cube.

Discussing Results

When the activity is finished, complete a class chart for everyone to see during the discussion. Discuss how length, area, and volume change at different rates. The following questions may be of use:

◆ What do you notice about your measurements?

◆ What patterns do you notice in the chart?

◆ What happens to the total surface area of all of the cubes as you cut smaller cubes?

The difference in the rate of change of areas and volumes that your students discover as they make smaller cubes is vital to understanding how scale affects structure for small objects.

What's Going On

Looking at individual cubes, you see that as the length of a side decreases, all linear dimensions decrease. Area shrinks faster. In the chart you can see that if a side length is halved, the area decreases by a factor of $\frac{1}{4}$. This is true of all areas: area of the base, total surface area, and area of a cross-section. If you decrease a side to one-fifth of the original length, the areas are $\frac{1}{125}$ times the original area. In general, if you make the sides of the cube $\frac{1}{n}$ times as big, than the areas are $\frac{1}{n} \times \frac{1}{n}$ or $\frac{1}{n^2}$ times as big. And volume decreases fastest of all. In the chart you can see that if the side length is halved, the volume decreases by a factor of $\frac{1}{8}$. If you decrease the side length to one-fifth, the volume is $\frac{1}{125}$ the original volume. In general, if you make the sides of the cube $\frac{1}{n}$ times as big, than the volume is $\frac{1}{n} \times \frac{1}{n} \times \frac{1}{n}$ or $\frac{1}{n^3}$ times as big.

As you move down in scale, length, area, and volume change at very different rates. Very small things have a lot of surface area for their volume or, more formally, a high surface-to-volume ratio. This has important physical conse-

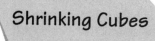
Shrinking Cubes

Length of Edge (fraction of big cube edge length)	Area of Base (fraction of big cube face area)	Area of Total Surface (fraction of big cube face area)	Volume (fraction of big cube volume)	Total Number of Cubes	Total Surface of all Cubes (in terms of big cube face area)
1	1	6	1	1	6
1/2	1/4	6/4	1/8	8	12
1/3	1/9	6/9 = 2/3	1/27	27	18
1/4	1/16	6/16 = 3/8	1/64	64	24
1/5	1/25	6/25	1/125	125	30
...	...	...	...	...	...

quences. For instance, a mouse is a very small warm-blooded animal. It has a relatively large surface (skin) over which to lose heat compared to a small volume in which to hold and generate heat. It has to eat a large amount of food to generate energy to make up for this lost body heat. (See the *Beyond This Book* section for more examples.)

It is also interesting to look at all of the cut cubes. When you look at things this way, you are keeping the total volume constant. As you cut the big cube into smaller cubes, you increase the amount of exposed surface area. The pattern of this increase is striking. When you cut cubes of one-half of the side length, the total surface area is two times as big. When you cut cubes of one-third of the side length, the total surface area is three times as big. In general, when you cut cubes of $\frac{1}{n}$ the side length, the total surface is *n* times as big. By cutting your big cube into smaller cubes, you increase the amount of surface for a fixed volume (i.e., for a fixed amount of clay.) This increase of surface has many physical consequences. For instance, we chew our food to break it into smaller pieces and increase the surface for a fixed volume. Increased surface speeds digestion. (See the *Beyond This Book* section for more examples.)

The geometry of the increase in total surface area is another interesting aspect of this activity. Why do three cuts of the cube through the center of the length, width, and height double the surface area? One way to think about it is to look at what happens when you make one cut. A cut creates a new surface. The new surface is the size of the existing face of the cube. Each cut actually creates two new surfaces, one on each side of the knife. Three cuts times two surfaces means that there are six new surfaces of the same size as the original cube's six surfaces. The new cubes, therefore, end up with double the total surface.

Extensions

◆ Start with two plasticene cubes about the same size. Ask the students how big the edge of a new cube will be if you cut one of the cubes in half and form it back into a cube. The edge of the new cube should be about 0.8 times the edge of the bigger cube. (Done exactly, the double-volume cube would have edges that are the cube root of half the length of the original sides.) This extension illuminates the difference between halving the volume of the cube, which is done here, and halving the linear dimensions. To halve the length, width, and height would remove seven-eighths of the clay, not just half.

◆ Make a sphere from about 8 ounces of clay. Ask the students how much clay it would take to make a sphere with half the circumference and half the diameter. Since these are both linear dimensions, the amount needed to halve diameter or circumference is the same. Halving the linear dimensions and keeping the shape the same is like halving the length, width, and height of a cube. It would take one-eighth the volume or one-eighth as much clay. In this case that would be one-sixteenth of a pound, or 1 ounce of clay.

Also, ask students how much smaller a sphere would be with half as much clay. This is analogous to the first extension of halving of the cube. In this case the diameter and circumference would be about 0.8 times as big.

Cylinders and Scale

TIME

◆ Two sessions of 45–60 minutes each

PREPARATION

◆ Set out materials.
◆ Find a place to store the materials between sessions.

GROUPING

◆ Pairs

MATERIALS
(per pair)

◆ Butcher paper (a few feet)
◆ One film canister
◆ One large, flat sheet of graph paper (centimeter paper works well)
◆ Scissors
◆ Scotch tape
◆ One pound of sand (for use in second session)
◆ One plastic picnic plate, aluminum pie pan or the like
◆ Optional: tagboard or old file folder
◆ Optional: compass
◆ One blank cylinders chart (from Appendix C)

TEACHER TIPS

◆ Cleanup is simplified if students work on paper when using the sand. The spilled sand can then easily be emptied into the wastebasket.

Context

Students need to see the patterns of scaled growth in different shapes before they can understand the universality of scaling patterns. In this activity, they can investigate the relative growth of lengths, areas, and volumes as cylinders are scaled up as they did with cubes in the *Growing Cubes* activity. However, in this case, we scale up by changing only the height of the cylinder and the diameter (or circumference) of the base. In the activity, students will measure the three linear dimensions of the cylinder. This is so that they will see that all linear dimensions increase at the same rate as you scale up proportionately. Similarly, they will be asked to measure two areas of the cylinder.

Students connect their experience with cylinders to the world outside the classroom by giving examples of where they encounter cylinders in their everyday life. These examples can include cans, poles, bottles, and pipes. Having students make a list of cylinders makes a nice homework assignment.

This activity should follow *Growing Cubes*.

What It Is

This activity requires a good deal of exacting work. It is best to do it in two sessions. In the first session, students will measure the cylinder's linear dimensions; in the second, they will measure for area and volume dimensions.

In the first session, begin by saying, "We have looked at the lengths, areas, and volumes of cubes and have seen the pattern as we doubled, tripled, and quadrupled the sizes of the cubes. Now we are going to try something similar with cylinders. As we build bigger cylinders, we will look at the growth in areas, volumes, and lengths. We will look for patterns in this growth and see how these patterns compare to the patterns we found with cubes." In starting this way, you are priming students to discover the amazing fact that the patterns here are exactly the same as in the cubes.

After illustrating how the cylinders are made (see below), have students predict what kind of pattern of growth they might expect as they scale up. How much like or unlike the patterns of cube growth do you expect the cylinder's pattern to be? Then, ask the students to make their cylinders in two steps. To build the cylinders, the students will draw and cut out rectangles of paper which will form the cylinder sides. To create a uniform basis for measurement in scaling, the students should use film canisters as the basis for what will be called the *unit rectangle*. The length and width of this unit rectangle will be doubled, tripled, quadrupled, etc., in the scaling-up process.

Making Cylinders

Step One

Start with lightweight writing paper. Cut out a rectangle slightly larger than that needed to make a match to the film canister cylinder. Roll this paper into a loose tube and put it *inside* the film canister. Let it expand so that it rests snugly against the inside of the canister, making sure that the bottom of the paper rests on the bottom of the canister. Now, mark a line along the top of the canister and mark another line where the edge of the paper overlaps itself. These marks define the edges of the unit rectangle. Cut out this rectangle.

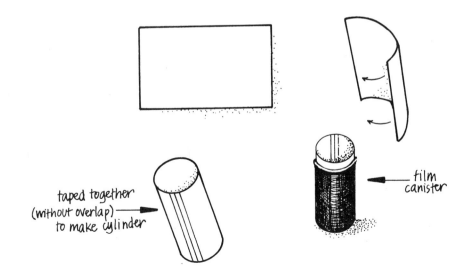

taped together
(without overlap)
to make cylinder

film canister

Step Two

After measuring the surface areas (see below), tape the longer sides of the rectangle together to form the cylinder. Tape so the edges just meet and do not overlap.

Cylinder Units of Measurement

The short length of the unit rectangle is the height of the cylinder, h. The longer length of the rectangle is the circumference of the cylinder, c. The area of the rectangle is then the area of the side of the cylinder. The volume of the cylinder is the amount of sand that it will hold.

Have the students make a number of scaled-up cylinders by doubling, tripling, etc., the height and circumference of the unit rectangle. Butcher paper works well for the double-, triple-, and quadruple-sized cylinders. Use stiffer tagboard or old file folders for the next few sizes. To make a doubled cylinder, one side of the rectangle is equal to $h \times 2$ and the other side is $c \times 2$ (see illustration). As students measure and cut out rectangles for larger cylinders, it is a good idea to have them trace their outlines on a sheet of chart paper before they tape them up into cylinders. This provides a convenient resource for comparison, measurements, and display of results. Some students have found it useful to have these outlines color-coded by size.

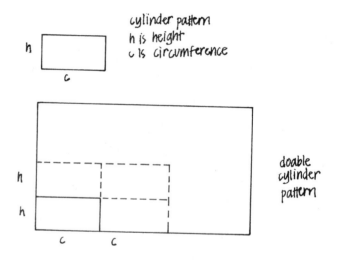

Measuring for Linear Dimensions

Each student group should start with a blank version of the chart shown below. In the first session, they measure the linear dimensions and the area of the sides. There are two ways to make these linear and area measurements. The first method has the students measuring the lengths in centimeters and the areas in number of square centimeters covered.

However, since students are measuring for purposes of comparison and to find growth patterns, it may be more useful to measure in another way. In the second method, students measure cylinder *height* in terms of h, the height of the smallest cylinder (which is also the short length of the *unit rectangle*); measure *circumference* in terms of c, the circumference of the smallest cylinder; and measure *diameter* of the base in terms of *d,* the diameter of the smallest cylinder. Given the way that the larger cylinders were constructed, measuring height and circumference in these units makes scaling patterns very clear. Diameters are determined by marking a *unit diameter* on the edge of a piece of paper held against the mouth of the film canister and placing marks adjacent to both of the inner sides. Measurement of the diameter of the base for larger cylinders then becomes equivalent to asking, "How many times does the unit diameter length fit into a line across the middle of a cylinder base?" Measuring the *area of the cylinder side* using this method is equivalent to asking the question, "How many small rectangles does it take to cover the larger rectangle which will form the side of the cylinder?" Results of all of these measurements should be recorded on the chart. Students answer this question using the manipulatives. We call these small rectangles *can surfaces,* since they represent the inner surface area of the film canister. These can surfaces are our unit of area.

Measuring for Area and Volume Dimensions

In the second session, the students will measure the area of the base and the volume and analyze and discuss results.

Since the base of the cylinder is a circle, areas are not simple. The best way to measure the *area of the base* is to outline the base on a piece of centimeter graph paper and count the squares enclosed.

Students measure volume using film canisters as their measuring cups. *Volume* is measured in terms of the number of film canisters full of sand (cans) that it takes to fill the cylinder. Start by placing the paper cylinder on a plastic picnic plate or something similar (so that the sand does not spill everywhere). One partner stands the cylinder on the plate, so that the plate forms a bottom, holding it in as round a shape as possible, and the other begins to pour in film canisters full of sand. As the sand goes in, its weight actually helps to make the cylinder round. If you are careful, very little sand will leak out of the bottom. Fill the cylinder to the top and record the number of cans that it holds.

Sometimes the question "If it isn't round does it change the volume?" will come up. Students can answer this by trying it. More noticeable changes in volume come from bigger changes in shape. In the extreme, the sides of the cylinder can be pushed together, reducing the volume to close to nothing.

Discussing Results

This part is similar to the *Discussing Results* section in the *Growing Cubes* activity. Tape sample cylinders of each size to your class chart. These will make the chart numbers more meaningful and guard against the problem of disconnecting the numbers from what they represent. Referring to your chart on the chalkboard, discuss the way that the linear measurements grow slowly, while the surface dimensions and volume grow more rapidly.

What's Going On

The scaling properties of the cylinder are the same as with the cubes. To grow larger cubes you have to change length, width, and depth, three linear dimensions. For the cylinder, you change two linear dimensions: the height and the circumference (or diameter of the base).

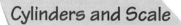

Cylinders and Scale

CYLINDERS CHART

Cylinder #	Height of Cylinder (h)	Diameter of base (d)	Circum- ference of base (c)	Area of base (cm²)	Area of cylinder surface (can surfaces)	Volume (cans)
1	1	1	1		1	1
2	2	2	2		4	8
3	3	3	3		9	27
4	4	4	4		14	64
5	5	5	5		25	125
...	...	...	...	...	...	...

The patterns observed here are the same as in *Growing Cubes*. See that activity and the overview of *The Mathematics of Scale* for more.

Extensions

◆ Instead of increasing all dimensions, try making cylinders with just double the height. Ask what happens to the volume (it doubles). Now try making a cylinder with double the circumference or diameter. Ask what happens to the volume (it is four times as big). Doubling the height doubles just one dimension of the cylinder. Doubling the circumference is like doubling the perimeter of the base on a cube. It doubles the length and width and increases the area of the base by four times. Also try tripling, quadrupling, etc., the height or circumference.

◆ See also Wings for Learning's *My Travels with Gulliver* (Appendix B).

Cones and Scale

TIME

◆ Two sessions of 45–60 minutes each

PREPARATION

◆ Make sets of tagboard circles of varying radii (e.g., 1, 2, 3, 4 . . . inches) for the groups to share. Students can use these as templates for tracing their own circles on butcher paper.
◆ Prepare blank cone charts (see materials list).
◆ Set out materials.
◆ Find a place to store the materials between sessions.

GROUPING

◆ Pairs

MATERIALS
(per pair)

◆ Butcher paper (several feet)
◆ Graph paper in flat sheets
◆ One blank cone chart (from Appendix C)
◆ Scissors
◆ Scotch tape
◆ Centimeter ruler
◆ String
◆ One pound of sand (for use in second session)
◆ Optional: compass

TEACHER TIPS

◆ Use the compasses to have the students draw their own paper circles, or
◆ Have the students trace precut tagboard circles onto butcher paper to make their own cutouts.

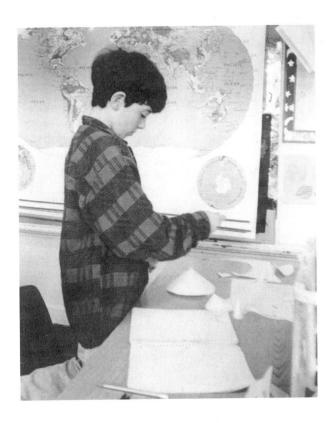

Context

Students need to see the patterns of scaled growth in different shapes before they can understand the universality of these scaling patterns. Here, as in *Growing Cubes,* students can investigate the relative growth of lengths, areas, and volumes as they scale up. This is an especially nice case, because we scale up by changing just one measurement, the radius of the circle from which the cone is made.

Since areas and volumes on the cone are not easily measured, students will have to gain some ease with estimation and finding approximate answers. The patterns that they find will be approximately like those for the cubes. If construction and measurements could be precise, the patterns would be exactly those of the cubes.

This activity should follow *Growing Cubes*. It should also follow *Cylinders and Scale* if you choose to do that activity. This order gives students sufficient experience with scale patterns to see the less precisely determined patterns in this activity.

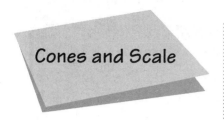

Cones and Scale

What It Is

Most teachers prefer to divide this activity into two sessions, one dealing with linear measurements and the second dealing with surface areas and volumes.

Constructing the Cones

Have the students trace and cut out different-sized circles on butcher paper and cut the circles exactly into halves. Tell them to tape together the two flat ends of one of the half-circles to form cones. They should be careful not to overlap the edges, but to butt them. Particularly for the cone with the 1-inch radius, try to measure and cut exactly—this cone will serve as the *unit cone* and will be used later for measuring. (You can also give the students sheets of paper with a compass and have them draw the circles and cut them out themselves, but this is sometimes difficult for younger students.) They should save the unused semicircles for later measurement of areas.

If you have several pairs of students sitting at tables together, you may want to give only one or two different sizes to each pair and have several pairs work together to cover all of the sizes.

Cone Units of Measurement

On chart paper or the chalkboard, draw a chart students can use for their measurements (see Appendix C). Alternatively, have students devise their own way to record the data.

Discuss with your students the meaning of each of the columns of the chart.

Explain to the students that the open circular end is the *base*—in other words, if the activity was not going to involve filling the cones, you could have them cover this hole with another piece of circular paper, and then the cone would be able to stand on this base.

Explain to the students the difference between the *length of the side* (a line measured along the side of the cone from the top of the cone to the bottom of the base) and the *height* (a line dropped from the center of the cone to the center of the base).

Measuring the Linear Dimensions

Ask the students to measure and chart the *linear dimensions* of the cones. If you have several pairs working in teams, each pair can fill in their findings on a shared chart. They can measure

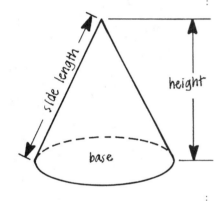

* length of the side
* height
* diameter of the "base"
* circumference of the "base."

The length, height, and diameter of the cone can be measured with a ruler. To measure the height, students should stand a ruler next to the cone and mark with their finger, or a straight object, where the height would meet the ruler. The easiest way to measure the circumference is to wrap a string around the base, mark the place where the string would begin to overlap itself, and then unwrap and measure that length of string. The cone is held in place while doing all of this by gently pushing down on it. Butcher paper holds up well under this stress.

As the students chart their findings, they will see that the linear dimensions of the different sizes grow together. In the cone made from a 2-inch-radius circle, the dimensions are about double those of the cone made from a 1-inch-radius circle. In the cone made from a 3-inch-radius circle, the dimensions are about triple those of the 1-inch cone. In general, when you enlarge something so that the proportions stay the same, all the lengths grow by the same factor.

You may want to end the first session here, storing the cones in a safe place.

Measuring for Area and Volume Dimensions

At the next session, ask the students to measure and chart the *surface dimensions* of the cone. To measure the area of the "base," they can draw its outline onto a flat sheet of graph paper and then count the number of squares on the sheet. To measure the surface area of the cone, they can take the unused half of the original circle, trace its outline on graph paper, and count the number of squares on that sheet. In this measurement of area, partial squares can be combined to get whole numbers.

When the students chart the dimensions of their various-sized cones, they will find that the growth of the surface dimensions is more rapid than the growth of the linear dimensions. When the results are charted, students will see that the surface dimensions of the cone made from a 2-inch-radius circle are about four times bigger than that of the cone made from a 1-inch-radius circle, while the cone made from a 3-inch-radius circle is about nine times bigger than the cone made from a 1-inch-radius circle. In general, areas grow as the square of linear dimensions (e.g., 2 times the length gives 2^2, or 4, times the area, and 3 times the length gives 3^2, or 9, times the area).

Ask the students to measure the volume of the cones. Have them fill the cone made from a 1-inch-radius circle with sand and use this as the standard of measurement. How many of these "conefuls" of sand are needed to fill a cone made from a 2-inch-radius circle? A 3-inch-radius circle cone? Have them first predict what they will find and then have them measure and chart the results; they will see that the growth of volume is the most extreme of all the measurements. The cone made from a 2-inch-radius circle holds about 8 times as much sand as the cone made from a 1-inch-radius circle. The cone made from a 3-inch-radius circle holds about 27 times as much sand as the cone made from a 1-inch-radius circle. In general, the volume grows as the cube of the linear dimensions (e.g., 2 times the length gives 2^3, or 8, times the volume; and 3 times the length gives 3^3, or 27, times the volume).

Discussing Results

This part is similar to the *Discussing Results* section in the *Growing Cubes* activity. Tape sample cones of each size to your class chart. These will make the chart numbers more meaningful and guard against the problem of disconnecting the numbers from what they represent. Referring to your class chart, discuss the way that the linear measurements grow slowly while the surface dimensions and

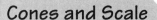

Cones and Scale

CONE CHART

Cone #	Length of cone side (cm)	Height of cone (cm)	Diameter of base (cm)	Circum- ference of base (cm)	Area of base (cm²)	Area of cone surface (cm²)	Volume (little cones)
1	2.5	2.2	2.5	8.0	5.1	10.1	1
2	5.1	4.4	5.1	16.0	20.3	40.5	8
3	7.6	6.6	7.6	23.9	45.6	91.2	27
4	10.2	8.8	10.2	31.9	81.1	162	64
5	12.7	11.0	12.7	39.9	127	253	125
6	15.2	13.2	15.2	47.9	182	365	216
7	17.8	15.5	17.8	55.8	248	497	343
8	20.3	17.7	20.3	63.8	324	649	512
9	22.9	19.9	22.9	71.8	410	821	729
10	25.4	22.1	25.4	79.8	507	1013	1000
. . .	. . .	. . .	. . .	. . .	. . .	. . .	. . .

Note: The measurements in this chart have been calculated more exactly than your classroom measurements will be.

volume grow more rapidly. Discuss the lack of precision in making and measuring cones as compared with cubes.

What's Going On

To understand the effects of scale on structure, it is essential to convince yourself that the kind of growth pattern we saw for lengths, areas, and volumes in cubes is a universal pattern for all scaled shapes. Looking at cones is a good exercise to help build that understanding. The scaling properties of cones are the same as with cubes. However, to grow larger cubes you have to change length, width, and depth—three linear dimensions. The cube growth patterns may seem like a special case. What makes cones particularly nice is that by changing just one linear measurement (the radius of the circle from which the cone is made), all of the other dimensions change automatically. For instance, if the radius of the circle doubles, all of the linear dimensions double, including the height of the cone, the circumference of the cone base, the diameter of the cone base, and the length of the cone side. The area of the base and the sloping surface both quadruple. The volume increases by a factor of 8.

Measurements and construction irregularities make the growth patterns in the cone charts less exact than those for cubes. Ideally, students will recognize that these patterns are like those that they saw in the cubes if the irregularities are removed.

Extensions

◆ Take a paper circle and, instead of cutting it perfectly in half, cut it in a greater or lesser amount (one-fourth, two-thirds, etc.). Now make a cone and measure and record the relationships. See also Wings for Learning's *My Travels with Gulliver* (Appendix B).

Fruit and Vegetable Area

TIME

◆ 30–60 minutes

PREPARATION

◆ Have students bring vegetable peelers and some produce from home.
◆ Copy blank charts (see materials list).
◆ Set out the materials.

GROUPING

◆ Pairs

MATERIALS
(per pair)

◆ Vegetable peeler
◆ Several types of produce (cucumbers, potatoes, apples, oranges) with skins clearly different from pulp
◆ Centimeter graph paper
◆ Two different-colored pencils
◆ Tall clear plastic container for submersing produce
◆ Measuring cup
◆ Optional: plastic wrap
◆ One or two blank fruit and vegetable measurement charts (see Appendix C)

TEACHER TIPS

◆ Cover the graph paper with plastic wrap to keep it from getting soggy.
◆ For each type of produce, get similarly shaped/different-sized items.
◆ Ask students to bring the produce from home.
◆ Use produce with skins that are markedly different from the pulp (e.g., oranges are good, but carrots are difficult).

Context

It's often easy to estimate the area of flat surfaces, but most things in the world are not flat. This activity gives students the chance to start to think about area in terms of everyday items such as fruits and vegetables. From there, they can apply their learning to trees and animals, even to their brothers and sisters. If you use similarly shaped fruits and vegetables of different sizes, you can also use this activity to study how area, volume, and area/volume ratios scale up and down.

This activity can be done at any point in your unit. However, students tend to notice more relationships between linear, surface, and volume dimensions after doing the *Cubes, Cones,* and *Cylinder* activities.

What It Is

First, review with the students how they have measured the areas of smooth-planed (flat-surfaced) objects such as squares and cubes. Then pose the question: "What is the surface area of your hand?" Students will typically estimate the length and width of their hand, forgetting about the skin in between their fingers. What about the surface area of your dog or cat?

Measuring Area

Have the students select one of the fruits or vegetables. Ask them to estimate in square centimeters the surface area of the selected produce. Have them draw the

Fruit and Vegetable Area

outline of the fruit or vegetable on graph paper. Next to this outline they should write what kind of produce they are working with, and they can record the length, width, and diameter of the object (they can count in terms of graph-paper squares).

Ask the students to peel the fruit or vegetable carefully in the longest, widest strips possible. But before they start, ask them to estimate how many squares of the graph paper the skin will cover. They can either outline an area on the paper or they can write down the number of squares that they expect the peels to cover. Have them go ahead and start peeling. When they are finished, have them lay out the strips on the graph paper, fitting the edges together wherever possible. By outlining all of the peels, they can then measure how many squares of the graph paper the skins have covered.

Students can also measure the cross-sectional area (e.g., the area of a slice of cucumber) by outlining a slice on the graph paper and counting the number of squares it covers.

Measuring Volume

Students can determine the volume of their produce using the displacement method. Put the fruit or vegetable into a tall container and add enough water to cover. They may have to hold the fruit or vegetable down with a pencil or fork. Mark the water level. Then remove the fruit or vegetable and mark the lower water level. You can measure the difference by pouring water from a measuring cup into your container until its water level is up to the high mark. The amount of water you pour in is equal to the volume of the fruit or vegetable.

If you have similarly shaped fruit and vegetables of different sizes you can look at how areas and volumes scale as the size changes. For example, suppose you have a small pickling cucumber and a large salad cucumber which is about three times as long and has a diameter about three times as wide. You will find for the large cucumber that all of the areas (the peel [surface] area and the cross-sectional area) are about nine times as big as they are for the small cucumber. (See *Concepts* in the overview of *The Mathematics of Scale* and/or *Cubes, Cylinders,* and *Cones* activities for explanations of these results.) When you use the water displacement method discussed above to measure the volume, you will find that the large cucumber's volume is about twenty-seven times greater than the small cucumber's volume.

Note that these measurements are approximate, so you should be looking for a ballpark result, rather than an exact one. The inexactitude is due to both the tools used for measurement and the slight variations inherent in non-manufactured materials.

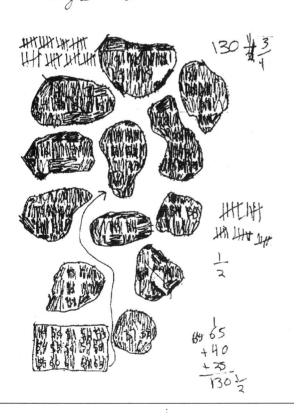

By Andy Birnbaum

Apple Graph game

This magnificant game tests your skill and your patience.

It is a game where you skin a medium sized apple put the skin on a centimeter graph paper and count how many squre centimers are in the skin. The average sqaure centimeter count is 130-135. One of the best things about this activity is that once the thing is over you get to eat what is left of the apple.

I reccomend this activity

P.S.

you can do this activity with oranges also.

$$130 \tfrac{3}{4}$$

$$\tfrac{1}{2}$$

$$\begin{array}{r} 65 \\ +40 \\ +25 \tfrac{1}{2} \\ \hline 130 \tfrac{1}{2} \end{array}$$

Discussing Results

Give students an opportunity to discuss their results in small groups, with partners, or to write in science journals before the whole-group discussion. When you move the conversations to the entire group, ask the students how they felt their predictions matched their results. Begin to discuss the concept of measuring surface areas of objects that are not flat. Discuss the surface area of the human body or of a bird's claw.

Ask why peeling the vegetable is a useful way of getting an approximate measure of its area. Ask what problems were encountered and solutions found during this process.

Ask how the results that they got here are related to the work in the *Cubes, Cylinders,* or *Cones* activities.

What's Going On

Area is more than just "length times width"—it is the amount of the surface. Similarly, volume exists for irregular as well as regular objects. Volume is the amount of space an object takes up. This activity helps students get a feel for these concepts.

The scaling part of this activity helps extend the *Cubes* and *Cones* concepts to real objects in the world. See the *Beyond This Book* section for more on this topic.

Extensions

- Try finding the areas of other objects, like your arm or a rubber glove, by covering it with regular squares made from masking tape. Invent other ways of measuring areas.

Perimeter/Area

TIME

◆ One or two 30–50 minute sessions

PREPARATION

◆ Cut string to length.
◆ Set out sugar cubes and graph paper.

GROUPING

◆ Individuals or pairs

MATERIALS
(per student or pair)

◆ 20-inch length of string or thread
◆ Centimeter graph paper
◆ A ruler
◆ 50–100 sugar cubes (sugar cubes are the cheapest way we have found of getting a large number of uniform cubes) or 50–100 paper squares
◆ Optional: 4 ounces plasticene (modeling clay) for extension

TEACHER TIPS

◆ This activity works best after the *Introduction to Cubes* activity.
◆ When working with sugar cubes, warn students about eating dirty cubes. To head off this problem, some teachers give each student one clean cube to eat before building.
◆ Cleanup is simplified if students work with their sugar cubes on paper. The loose sugar granules can then easily be emptied into the wastebasket.

Context

When investigating the mathematics of scale and structure, the relationship between the area and the volume of three-dimensional objects often comes into play. Students can begin to get a feel for this by investigating the analogous relationship between perimeter and area in two-dimensional objects.

There may be a good deal of confusion about this relationship, mostly around the idea that a figure with a small area can have a large perimeter. Even the idea of what is meant by perimeter and area can be difficult.

It is useful to bring in examples from students' experiences to clarify these concepts. For perimeter, you can talk about how much fencing it takes to enclose different-sized and -shaped yards or how long a string of Christmas lights it takes to encircle a house. Area can be discussed in terms of how much material is needed to cover or blanket an object—for instance, how many classroom carpets it would take to cover the playground. Real-life examples engage the students' preexisting knowledge and help them to integrate what they learn into their previous experience.

What It Is

There are two parts to this activity. The first involves looking at the different areas that you can get with a fixed perimeter. The second involves looking at different perimeters that you can get with a fixed area.

Perimeter/Area

Part 1: Fixed Perimeter

For each student or group, use one 20-inch length of string, a ruler, and a sheet of graph paper.

Start by discussing the idea of perimeter and area with your students. If you have not done much previous work on this topic you may need an extensive number of examples. Draw an irregular figure on a large sheet of graph paper and show how string can be used to measure its perimeter (i.e., run the string along the outline of the figure, taping it periodically to hold it in place. Then pull the string straight to measure the perimeter. It is fun to have the students guess how long it will be before you straighten the string.) The area of the figure can be found by determining how many squares on the graph paper are enclosed. You will have to approximate since only parts of some squares are involved.

Next, hand out the string, ruler, and graph paper to the students. Have them tie the two ends of the string together to form a complete loop. The length of string in this loop will be the fixed perimeter of the figures that the students form. Have your students measure the length of the string in the loop. They will probably figure out that this measurement can be made by stretching the loop so that it forms two adjacent strings, measuring the length and multiplying by two. Ask your students to use their loop of string to make several rectangles on the graph paper. They should try "skinny" rectangles and not-so-skinny rectangles. Have the students record length, width, and area (i.e., the number of squares enclosed) of each shape right on the drawing. Prompt your students to look at these questions:

◆ Which rectangle has the smallest area? (the skinniest)

◆ Which rectangle has the largest area? (the square)

After looking at rectangles ask:

◆ What other type of shape would have the largest area? (the circle)

Part 2: Fixed Area

For each student or group, use a set of sugar cubes or paper squares.

In this activity, students build with sugar cubes without stacking them on top of each other but by covering squares of graph paper in a two-dimensional direction. Therefore, each set of cubes, while creating different shapes, will cover the same number of squares and thus have the same area.

It is very helpful if students have done the *Introduction to Cubes* activity before this part of the activity. If so, they can use the same length and area units created in that activity. If not, read the following inset.

It is useful to establish units of convenience for working with these cubes in this activity. You and your class can invent your own names for these units based on the dimensions of the sugar cube. We came up with units as follows:

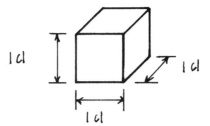

Length: The natural unit of length is the length of the edge of the sugar cube. We called this unit the *cube length*, or *cl*. The perimeter of a single sugar cube is 4 cl's.

Area: The natural unit of area is the surface covered by one face of the sugar cube. We call this unit the *face*. The total surface area of a single sugar cube is 6 faces.

If your students have not done the *Introduction to Cubes* activity, give them five minutes to create any shaped figure and then have them figure out perimeter and area for that figure.

All students or pairs should have the same number of cubes so that they can compare their results. The more cubes the students have to work with, the more interesting and diverse will be the shapes they create. If possible, supply each student or group with 50 to 100 cubes, but you can get by with as few as 36 if necessary. Make sure the rules for building are clear.

◆ Build one layer high only. No stacking!

◆ Cubes must be touching whole edge to whole edge. No corner-to-corner touching and no partial overlaps!

Start by asking the students to find the figure with the smallest perimeter. After some time they will find that figures that are most like squares have the smallest perimeter. Ask the students to report their smallest perimeters. If some have very different answers from the rest, have their results checked by other students. Ask your students why they think that the squares have smaller perimeters than the rectangles made with the same number of sugar cubes. Some may see that more sugar cubes are on the inside, away from the square's edges.

Next, ask your students to make the figure with the largest possible perimeter. Again, ask students to report their results. Many are pretty savvy about this now and build a "worm," a long straight line of cubes. *This has the maximum perimeter, which is equal to two times the number of sugar cubes plus two.* Students can see this by noticing that each sugar cube in the line has two sides exposed and that each of the cubes on the ends of the line has another side exposed.

Finally, ask your students to make a figure with a large perimeter but set a limit on the amount of space that they can use—for instance, restrict them to working on only half a sheet of paper (they can fold the sheet in half). Or you could use the string loop from the *Fixed Perimeter* activity to form a boundary which sets the limits of the working space. Student solutions to this challenge are very interesting, and they may want to record them by drawing. Some students try spirals. Others make figures that look like combs or branching trees. These figures have a number of natural analogs that can be referenced. (See *What's Going On* below.)

Discussing Results

Part 1: Fixed Perimeter

Reproduce a few of the students' rectangles on the board. Label the length, width, and area for each and make sure you include a square. Remind your students that all of the figures have the same perimeter. Start the discussion with a question like, "What do the figures with particularly large or small areas look like?" They will notice that the thin rectangles have small areas and the square has a larger area.

Ask them, "What figure has the largest area?" The circle has the largest area. However, what is most important here is your students' reasoning. Ask your students to say why they think their answers are correct. Have them discuss why they think that thin figures have small areas, and squares and circles have large areas. There is often a great deal of confusion between perimeter and area. You may hear comments during some activities that suggest that students believe they can determine area by measuring the distance around something. This activity is designed to confront that student confusion.

The most fundamental idea to elicit from students is that for a particular (fixed) perimeter there can be a large variety of areas and that the area depends on shape. Another important idea is that "skinny" shapes have small areas and "fat" shapes have large areas.

Part 2: Fixed Area

In this part of the activity, you should stop at several points along the way for discussion (see *What It Is* above). After making figures with small and large perimeters, help the students to generalize by asking, "What do the structures with particularly large or small perimeters look like?"

The discussion of student solutions to the figure with a large perimeter in a confined space can be very interesting. Ask students to report on their results and to show their figures. Ask what strategy they were using to solve the problem. Some of the figures may get increased perimeter by putting the sugar cubes slightly out of alignment. You will want to discuss whether or not this is fair. Discussion can lead to examples in the natural world of things with relatively large surfaces for their volume. (See *What's Going On* below.)

What's Going On

In Part 1, students worked with a fixed perimeter. In that case, the amount of area enclosed depended on the shape. As shapes get thinner the area enclosed decreases until, in the extreme case of opposite sides' touching, there is no area enclosed. As the edges of shapes move away from each other, the area enclosed increases. To get the most area enclosed, the circle works best.

In Part 2, students worked with fixed areas. In that case, the perimeter depended on the shape. The more cube edges that can be "buried" inside the figure, the fewer edges there are to contribute to the perimeter on the outside. The square does this best and has the smallest perimeter. To get large perimeters, you do just the opposite: you want as many edges as possible exposed to the outside. A long "worm" does this well.

Making large perimeters in confined spaces has many analogs in our world. For instance, if ships in a harbor docked directly along the shore, there would be a very limited number of ships that could dock at one time. Building piers that jut out into the water increases the perimeter of the docks and allows more ships to dock at one time. The outline of the piers jutting out from a shore may resemble some of your students' solutions to the problem of making large perimeters in a confined space.

If we move everything up one dimension, there are innumerable other examples of structures that look like your students' figures in the human and natural world. In this case, we are looking at structures with relatively large surface areas for a given volume. One example can be found in towels. A towel absorbs water across the surface of its threads. Fluffy towels are more absorbent because they have a larger surface area of thread than flatter towels. Another example can be found in the root of a tree. A tree needs a great deal of water to supply its vast volume. Water enters a tree across the surface of the root. To get more water, trees have evolved intricate sets of branching roots and root hairs to increase root surface area. Lungs have evolved in a similar fashion to increase the surface area in contact with the air we breath. In an automobile, the engine heats up and is cooled by flowing water. The water releases heat to the air across the surface of the pipes through which it flows. Car radiators are designed with narrow pipes that wind back and forth to increase the surface area through which heat can flow. All of these designs are mirrored by the figures that your students create.

Extension

◆ You can extend these ideas to three dimensions by working with a fixed amount of clay. Give each student or pair about 4 ounces of clay. Ask students to make the shape with the smallest surface area. If your students are extending their learning from the two-dimensional case, they will make cubes, or cubelike cylinders or spheres. In this case, the sphere has the smallest surface area for a given volume. Also, ask your students to make a shape with a large surface area. You will probably see pancake and worm shapes as answers to this question. Most of your students will realize that the thinner you get the clay, the more surface you get. In both instances, the discussion of why they think their shape answers the challenge is critical to building their understanding.

PART THREE

The Effect of Scale on Structure

Note to the Teacher

The following conceptual overview is for you. Its purpose is to provide you with a conceptual framework for organizing your teaching and responding to student discoveries. For your students, developing an understanding of these ideas will grow out of experiencing the phenomena which are inherent in the activities.

You should not feel that you have to understand all of this information before you start teaching. Try these activities along with your students, using this conceptual overview as your own reference. Engaging in the activities will clarify many of the concepts for you as well as for your students.

Context

We are all used to dealing with materials on a scale corresponding to our experience of these materials in everyday life. On this scale, steel is hard and rigid, rock is solid and immobile, and when you turn off the motor on a boat the propeller gradually slows down and it glides to a stop. But if you change the scale, all of this can change. Large steel suspension bridges can sway and buckle in the wind like pieces of fabric. In a large enough rock mountain, and over long periods of time, the rock on the bottom gives and flows like very slow molasses. When small, one-celled animals in water stop moving their propelling flagella, they stop moving immediately—no gradual slowing down, no gliding to a stop.

What happens when we look at things on a scale outside our everyday experience? What things change and what things remain the same? In the *Mathematics of Scale* section, we looked at the mathematics of scale change. We can use such mathematics to help us understand the change and invariance with scale that we observe in the structures we build.

The activities in the *Physics and Engineering of Structures* section gave students a good feel for materials and the key properties of structure. In the *Effect of Scale on Structure* section, we are concerned with these properties at different scales.

◆ How are structural properties affected by scaling up or down?

◆ What qualities change and what qualities are independent of size?

◆ How do you change your structures when you enlarge or shrink them? Which of these changes are necessary to keep your structures standing? What new things are possible that weren't before?

These are the questions that are explored in this section. The activities are designed to give students experiences of scale change so that they can begin to form an understanding of structural change due to a change of scale.

You can build on your students' construction experiences from the *Physics and Engineering of Structures* activities by having them build similar structures with similar materials at different scales. In this section, we will provide several detailed activities to illustrate this process and a number of suggestions for additional scaling tie-ins to earlier activities.

In addition, there are a number of activities involving water and surface tension where the effects of changing size on structure are speedily and clearly manifest. Some teachers have interspersed these activities among the building activities from this section to begin to introduce the idea of changes in structure as size changes.

Concepts

How does scale affect structure? The various elements of structure are dependent on different dimensions, and they change differently with scale. For instance, heat flow depends on surface area of a body. The lift of a bird's wing depends on its area. The rate at which your body consumes oxygen depends on its volume. The most important elements in our look at physical structures are *strength* and *mass* (or *weight*). Strength for a fixed material depends on cross-sectional or surface area. Mass, on the other hand, depends on volume.

A good example of these dependencies is the case for why there can be no giants as they are portrayed in fairy tales. The strength of a person's bone depends on the cross-sectional area of that bone. If you double the thickness of the bone (the diameter), then it has four times the area and is four times as strong; meanwhile, the volume (and therefore weight) will have increased by a factor of 8.

Imagine this: scale up a human being to be a giant, retaining all of the same proportions as an average-sized human. In *Honey, I Blew Up the Kids,* a $2\frac{1}{2}$-foot infant is enlarged to a height of 20 feet. He is scaled up proportionately to 8 times his normal size. This means his feet are 8 times longer, his hair is 8 times longer, and his hat size (circumference of his head) is 8 times larger. On the other hand, his area dimensions (including bone and muscle cross-section, etc.) have increased by a factor of 64 (8^2)—he's 64 times stronger.

However, before you worry about the destructive potential of this kid on the loose, look at his volume (weight), which has increased by a factor of 512 (8^3). If he started out at 35 pounds, he has blown up to 17,920 pounds, almost 9 tons. Each little section of bone (of which there is 64 times more than before) has to support 8 times as much weight as before. His bones would snap under his own weight.

How does nature deal with these issues? Look at the legs of a mouse and compare them with the legs of an elephant. The mouse's leg is much thinner in proportion to its body than is the elephant's. This is an effect of scale on structure: the elephant needs thicker legs to support a greater weight, and it needs thicker muscles and thicker bones than a mouse.

Think about trees: the giant redwood's trunk is proportionately much thicker than that of a smaller Douglas fir. This is because of the additional weight the redwood has to carry. There are also geological consequences. Limited mountain height is due to scale effects. A 5,000-foot mountain is common. A 20,000-foot mountain of the same shape is four times as tall. The area of the base of the mountain is 16 times (4^2) as great, but the volume and hence the weight of the mountain is 64 times (4^3) as large. Each square foot of base has to support 4 times as much weight as in the 5,000-foot mountain. As mountains get bigger, the weight per unit on the base continues to increase. Eventually it gets so great that it causes the rock at the base to become ductile and flow outward, effectively limiting the mountain's height.

The same physics applies to the mountains on the planet Mars; but since Mars is a smaller planet with less gravitational attraction, the tallest mountains on Mars are taller than those on Earth.

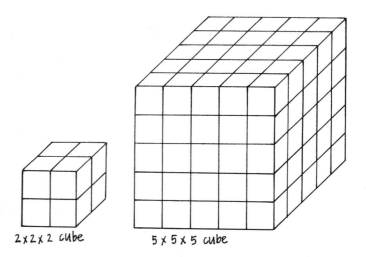

2 x 2 x 2 cube   5 x 5 x 5 cube

Look again at the cube. In a 2-by-2-by-2 cube, each cube on the base supports the weight of one cube on top of it. If you take the same material, but scale it up to be a 5-by-5-by-5 cube, you find that each base cube must support the weight of four other cubes. This is one of the consequences of scaling up: things become heavy very quickly.

Scaling down also has important structural consequences. As you scale down proportionately, volume shrinks much faster than area. If a 50-inch-tall child shrank down to 5 inches tall, $\frac{1}{10}$ her original size, her muscle cross-sectional area would be $\frac{1}{100}$ ($\frac{1}{10^2}$) its original size, so she would be 100 times weaker. But her volume would be $\frac{1}{1000}$ ($\frac{1}{10^3}$) of the original, so she would be 1,000 times as light. Ounce for ounce she would be 10 times stronger than she was before. If the full-size girl could jump half her height before shrinking, she could now jump 5 times her height. If she could lift 75 percent (or .75) of her full-size weight, she could now lift 750 percent (or 7.5) times her shrunken weight.

If you scale down far enough, surface increases so much compared to volume that weight becomes insignificant compared to intermolecular forces between surface molecules. In the world of the microbe, surface tension, cohesion, and viscosity play key roles as physical forces. Weight can be ignored. The mathematics of scaling down is explored in the *Shrinking Cubes* activity.

We see these effects very clearly in several of our activities. In *Exploring Water Drops,* we see that the small drops are spherical but the large drops are flat. Here, strength depends on surface tension, and, hence, surface area and weight depend on volume. The larger drops have too much weight for the surface tension to pull into a sphere. In the *Clay Beams and Columns* activity, we have a very straightforward illustration of volume and weight growing faster than cross-sectional area and strength.

This book focuses on scale effects on the weight and strength of materials. But the effects of scale differences are much broader than that. For examples of some of these broader effects, see *Beyond This Book* at the end of this section.

Skewers and Garden Poles—Building Up

TIME

- 45 minutes for exploration
- 1–2 hours for building

PREPARATION

- Bundle skewers and tape for each group.

GROUPING

- Pairs, or groups of four to five

MATERIALS
(per group)

- 35–60 9-inch bamboo skewers (available at grocery stores) (8-inch skewers will also work)
- One roll of $\frac{1}{8}$-inch masking tape (available at auto detailing supply stores) or $\frac{1}{4}$-inch tape
- Optional: 10 weights (e.g., large washers or film canisters filled with sand)
- Optional: paper clips

TEACHER TIPS

- Find a space to store skewer structures for later comparison with larger structures.
- See *Garden Poles—Building Up* for larger-scale materials.

Context

This activity is a scaled-down version of the *Garden Poles—Building Up* activity found in the *Physics and Engineering of Structures* section. If you have previously done that activity, you may want to repeat it after trying the skewer activity to emphasize the effects of changing scale. Since both sizes are made from bamboo, you eliminate the variable of a different material, which allows your students to attribute the differences that they notice to the change in scale. The 9-inch bamboo skewers are about one-sixth of the length of the bamboo garden poles. They are also about one-sixth as thick. (Note that there is some irregularity in the larger bamboo garden poles which may raise some questions. Ask your students what can be attributed to the pole irregularity and what to the scale change.)

What It Is

Initiate the building with skewers in the same manner as you do the garden poles. The students need some time to get familiar with working with skewers and tape.

During the first session of 45 minutes, ask the students to build a self-standing structure using 35 skewers and masking tape. Give them the following rules for building:

♦ The tape can only be wrapped twice around any given joint or stick.

♦ When joining sticks in a straight line, the sticks may only be taped together at two points (at each of these points, the piece of tape may only be wrapped around twice).

garden poles taped together in two spots

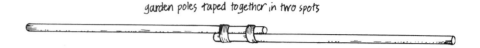

For the second session, use the same building rules as before, and challenge the students to do one of the following:

♦ Build a structure that is taller than it is wide.

♦ Build a structure 13 inches tall that will hold about one-sixth of the weight of a book. (Discuss with your students that this activity is a scaled-down version of the *Garden Poles—Building Up* activity. Heights are one-sixth of the corresponding garden pole tower height. But should the weight you are trying to support be one-sixth of that used for the garden pole tower? Or should it correspond to the reduction in volume, i.e., $\frac{1}{216}$ (or $\frac{1}{6 \times 6 \times 6}$ of the larger scale weight)?

♦ Using a maximum of 60 skewers, build a structure 2 feet tall. Additions to this may include asking, "Which group can do this using the fewest number of skewers?" and "Which group can build the tallest tower?"

♦ Challenge the students to build a 2-foot structure (using 60 skewers) which can hold at least a $\frac{1}{6}$-pound load (or a smaller load, like a paper clip). After they have completed their structures, add $\frac{1}{6}$-pound weights (or more paper clips) one at a time. As the structure starts to respond to the load (by leaning, compressing, or swaying), have the students predict how many more weights the structure will hold and how the structure will break.

These challenges are scaled-down versions of the garden pole activities with all of the lengths and weights divided by 6. Discuss with your students whether or not they think this is the proper way to scale down the challenge. The work on two scales is most instructive if student groups work on the same challenge on both the large and small scale. If they build on the small scale first, they could start on the large scale by trying to replicate their design. This is very instructive as it is usually impossible to replicate the small scale design exactly.

As with the garden poles, choose the difficulty of the challenge based on the age and the level of building skills of your students. It is especially important in this activity to be sensitive to the issue of creating winners and losers. Student groups put a lot of time and effort into these structures and may feel bad if their tower doesn't measure up. Setting a challenge level which most students can meet and allowing them to go beyond this level is one useful strategy. Look for various criteria to judge buildings, including the degree of risk, stability, and innovation.

A particularly important criteria for these structures is aesthetics. Aesthetics is not just how pretty a structure is but also how it makes the viewer feel. Does the structure seem heavy? Is it open, light, and airy? Does it create a feeling of tension, as if something is about to happen any second? Does it create an image of movement? These skewer structures may be considered sculptures and looked at in those terms. Working on two scales offers the opportunity to discuss how the aesthetic considerations are affected by a change in scale. Does an unstable, wavering, big tower create a different feel than a little one? Do your ideas of shapes that are pleasing change with size? These kinds of questions can lead to the realm of architecture and the role that scale plays in design.

Discussing Results

After the session with the skewers, have the students share their results with the whole class. Ask the same sorts of questions as in the work with garden poles. Record their discoveries on the chalkboard or chart paper; students may also record drawings of structures, observations, and questions in their science logs.

◆ What happened when they were building?

◆ What did they find out about building with these materials?

◆ What difficulties did they encounter and how did they resolve them?

◆ How would they build their towers differently if they were to do it again?

The final building session is followed by weight testing, measurement, and discussion.

◆ What physical phenomena did they observe?

◆ If their structure was wobbly, how did they stabilize it?

With structures that are tested with weights, raising questions like the following can help students see some of the physical implications of what they are doing:

◆ How many weights can be hung before the structure collapses?

◆ Does it matter where the weights are hung?

◆ Will the structure be more likely to collapse if the weights are hung in one place or spread out?

◆ Predict where the structure will weaken first. Can that area be strengthened so that another area will collapse first?

Questions about which poles are being bent and where poles are being pulled out of their taped joints help emphasize the concepts of tension and compression in these structures. (See the overview of *The Physics and Engineering of Structure* for background on these concepts.)

The following questions will help to elucidate the aesthetic qualities of a student's work.

◆ Did you have a design or shape in mind before you started or did it evolve as you worked?

◆ What pleases you most about the design of your structure? Why?

♦ What other structures or places does your structure bring to mind?

♦ What kind of feelings does your structure evoke? Does it suggest peace, tension, humor, or excitement?

♦ Talk about how the use of balance and movement in your structure affects the feel of the structure.

♦ Pick a good name for your structure.

Discussing Scale Differences

Finally, ask your students what was different in building on the two different scales. What was the same? The following questions can encourage further thinking and discussion:

♦ Were there any surprises in going from one scale to another?

♦ On which scale was it easier to work? Which was harder? In what ways?

♦ What problems were encountered at both scales? What things did you have problems with at one scale but not the other?

♦ What things did you learn on one scale that turned out not to be true on the other scale?

♦ On which scale were structures most stable? Why do you think this was so?

♦ On which scale were structures easier to balance? Why do you think this was so?

♦ On which scale were structures more rigid? On which more floppy?

♦ On which scale did the taped joints hold together best? Why do you think this was so?

♦ How is the "feel" of the large tower different from that of the small tower?

♦ What is it about the small and large towers that creates a different reaction or impression in the viewer?

After a good deal of discussion, a simple demonstration is helpful. Tape four skewers together with overlapped joints to form a piece about 24 inches long. Tape four garden poles together with lapped joints to form a piece about 14 feet long. Now try to lift these pieces by holding on to the ends. The skewers will lift easily and stay fairly rigid. The garden poles will be difficult to lift and will bend significantly. Ask your students how this connects to what they saw in their structures.

What's Going On

Building on two scales gives clear examples of how some relationships of physical properties change with scale and others remain the same. On both scales, triangular elements were the most stable. However, structures seemed less stable and less rigid on the larger scale.

The proportions of the skewers and the garden poles were the same. (This means that if the skewers are 200 times as long as they are thick, then the garden poles are also 200 times as long as they are thick.) The linear dimensions of the garden poles are 6 times the size of the corresponding linear dimensions of the skewers.

This means the garden pole areas are 36 (6^2) times larger than the skewer areas. The garden pole volume is 216 (6^3) times larger than the skewer volume. The physical consequences of this are dramatic. Strength depends on cross-sectional area. This means garden poles are 36 times as strong as skewers. However, weight depends on volume. Garden poles weigh 216 times as much as skewers. Garden poles structures have to support greater weight for their strength and are therefore more floppy.

There are other scaling consequences as well. Since garden pole towers are much taller than skewer towers, any slight lean moves the garden pole tower's center-of-mass farther than the same degree lean would for a skewer tower whose center-of-mass is closer to its base. This makes the tower less stable. Also, weights added to garden pole towers are much farther from the base, which causes even greater instability.

Extensions

◆ **Tie-in to the *Straw and Pins—Building Up* activity:** This activity can be scaled up significantly by using plastic golf tubes and nails or wire. Plastic golf tubes are sold in some shops that carry golf supplies. They have $1\frac{1}{2}$-inch diameters and are as long as the shaft of a golf club. A set of these is rather expensive. If you use them, you will probably just get one set for the class. To get repeated use, try putting holes in the tubes with a hole punch and joining the tubes with wire. The same activity can be scaled down by using cocktail straws and the smallest pins available at a sewing store. The scale change is not large, but the effects are still noticeable.

◆ **Tie-in to the *Toothpicks and Clay* activity:** This activity can be scaled up by working with skewers and clay or small wooden dowels and clay. Have students experiment with the size of the clay joints to see what works best. Scaling this up with clay joints may be frustrating. You may want to try using toothpicks and miniature marshmallows to start with and then scale up using full-size marshmallows. It is difficult to scale down with this activity. If you would like to try, have your students break off the pointed ends of toothpicks and use them to build.

◆ **Tie-in to the *Clay Towers* activity:** This activity lends itself very well to illustrating the effects of scale on structure. The first two extensions in this activity lead to considerations of scale.

1. Have the students predict the results if the amount of clay were doubled. One third grader commented in her picture-report that it would not be possible to make a tower of twice the clay twice as tall, because too much would have to be used to make the base "sterdy," thus limiting the height. Another predicted that with twice the clay he could construct a tower one and a half times the height of his current tower. Ask the students to test their predictions with double the clay. This extension introduces the key idea that you cannot always keep the same shape (proportions) when you scale up.

2. Have the students predict the results if more or less clay is used. Try half as much. Try one-tenth. How about six times as much? Ask the students to test their predictions with clay. They will have to combine their clay with that of others to test the larger predictions.

See the *Clay Beams and Columns* activity for more on scaling with clay.

Skewers and Garden Poles—Building Out

TIME

- 45 minutes for exploration
- 1–2 hours for building

PREPARATION

- Bundle skewers and tape for each group.

GROUPING

- Four to five, or pairs

MATERIALS
(per group)

- 35 9-inch bamboo skewers (available at grocery stores) (8-inch skewers will also work)
- One roll of $\frac{1}{8}$-inch masking tape (available at auto detailing supply stores) or $\frac{1}{4}$-inch tape
- 1 to 2 feet of duct tape
- Optional: 10 weights to be shared by several groups (e.g., large washers or film canisters filled with sand)

TEACHER TIPS

- Make some space to store skewer structures for later comparison with larger structures.
- See *Garden Poles—Building Out* for larger-scale materials.

Context

This activity is a scaled-down version of the *Garden Poles—Building Out* activity found in the *Physics and Engineering of Structures* section. If you have previously done that activity, you may want to repeat it after trying the skewer activity to emphasize the effects of changing scale. The 9-inch bamboo skewers are about one-sixth the linear dimensions of the garden poles.

What It Is

Initiate the building with skewers in the same manner as you did the garden poles. The students need some time to get familiar with working with skewers and tape. If this is your students' first use of skewers, start with a 45-minute session in which students are asked to build a self-standing structure using 35 skewers and masking tape. Give them the following rules for construction:

- The tape can only be wrapped twice around any given joint or stick.

- When joining sticks in a straight line, the sticks may only be taped together at two points (at each of these points, the piece of tape may only be wrapped around twice).

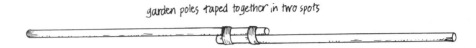

garden poles taped together in two spots

For the next session, introduce the cantilever. A cantilever is a projecting beam or other structure which is supported at only one end (e.g., awnings, flagpoles, tree limbs). Challenge your students to build a cantilever out from a wall or out from a tabletop. Use the same rules for building as above with the following addition:

- Sticks may be taped to the wall or tabletop with a reasonable amount of duct tape.

Challenge the students to do one of the following:

- With 35 skewers, how far out from the wall or tabletop can you build a structure?

- Can you build a cantilever 22 inches out from the wall or table?

- What is the strongest cantilever you can build 14 inches out from a wall or tabletop?

- Can you build a cantilever 18 inches out from the wall or table that will hold one large paper clip?

These challenges are scaled down versions of the *Garden Poles—Building Out* activities with all of the lengths and weights divided by six. Discuss with your students whether or not they think this is the proper way to scale down the challenge. The work on two scales is most instructive if student groups work on the same challenge on both the large and small scale. If they build on the small scale first, they could start on the large scale by trying to replicate their design. This is very instructive as it is usually impossible to replicate the small scale design exactly.

As with the garden poles, choose the difficulty of the challenge based on the age and level of building skills of your students. It is especially important in this activity to be sensitive to the issue of creating winners and losers. Student groups put a lot of time and effort into these structures and may feel bad if their structure doesn't measure up. Setting a challenge level which most students can meet and allowing them to go beyond this level is a useful strategy. Look for various criteria to judge buildings, including the degree of risk, stability, and innovation.

The question of rules and what is fair inevitably arises in these challenges. Typical questions are, "How do you measure distance from the wall or tabletop?" and "Are the structures allowed to droop, and if so, how much?" Setting rules by class discussion enhances sensitivity to these problems. "Where is it fair to hang the weights?" is another question that often arises. The place where weights are hung is critical for cantilevers. When we hear students protest "it's not fair" when a group hangs their weight in close to the wall or table, we know that they understand an important aspect of torque.

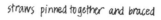

Skewers and Garden Poles—Building Out

As in the *Garden Poles—Building Out* activity, aesthetics is a particularly important criteria for these structures. Aesthetics is not just how pretty a structure is but also how it makes the observer feel. Is the structure rigid and strong looking? Does it have a pleasing curve to it? Is it open, light, and airy? Does it create a feeling of tension, as if something were about to happen any second? Does it create an image of movement? These skewer structures may be considered sculptures and looked at in those terms. Working on two scales offers the opportunity to discuss how the aesthetic considerations are affected by change in scale. Does a long cantilever which wavers and twists create a different feel than a short one? Do your ideas of shapes that are pleasing change with size? These kinds of questions can lead to the realm of architecture and the role that scale plays in design.

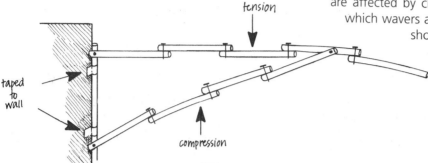

straws pinned together and braced

tension

taped to wall

compression

Discussing Results

After the session with the skewers, have the students share their results with the whole class. Ask the same sorts of question as in the work with garden poles. Record their discoveries on the chalkboard or on chart paper; students may also record drawings of structures, observations, and questions in science logs.

- ◆ What happened while building?

- ◆ What difficulties did they encounter and how did they resolve them?

- ◆ What questions do they have as a result of the activity?

The final building session is followed by weight testing, measurement, and discussion.

- ◆ What physical phenomena did they observe?

- ◆ If their structure was wobbly, how did they stabilize it?

Often when building cantilevers, the problem of twisting to one side or the other arises. This is less pronounced on this smaller scale but should be looked for so it can be compared to the larger-scale structures.

Most of these cantilever structures will not hold much weight. In structures that are tested with weights, raising questions like the following can help the students see some of the implications of what they are doing:

- ◆ How many large paper clips can be hung before the structure collapses?

- ◆ Does it matter where the weights are hung?

- ◆ Will the structure be more likely to collapse if the weights are hung in one place or spread out?

- ◆ Predict where you think the structure will weaken first. Can that area be strengthened so that another area will collapse first?

Questions about where skewers are being bent or pulled out of their taped joints help locate the tension and compression elements in these structures. Often, a long line of skewers at the top of a structure will be in tension and a long line of skewers along the bottom will be in compression (see illustration, facing page).

The following questions will help to elucidate the aesthetic qualities of a student's work:

◆ Did you have a design or shape in mind before you started or did it evolve as you worked?

◆ What pleases you most about the design of your structure? Why?

◆ What other structures or places does your structure bring to mind?

◆ What kind of feelings does your structure evoke? Does it suggest peace, tension, humor, or excitement?

◆ Talk about how the use of balance and movement affects the feel of the structure.

◆ Pick a good name for your structure.

Discussing Scale Differences

Finally, ask your students what was different in building cantilevers on the two different scales. How were they the same? The following questions can encourage further thinking and discussion:

◆ Were there any surprises in going from one scale to another?

◆ On which scale was it easier to work? Which was harder? In what ways?

◆ What problems encountered were the same at both scales? What things did you have problems with at one scale but not the other?

◆ What things did you learn on one scale that turned out not to be true on the other scale?

◆ On which scale did cantilevers twist to the side most? Why do you think this was so?

◆ On which scale were structures easier to keep from drooping? Why do you think this was so?

◆ On which scale were structures more rigid? On which more floppy?

◆ On which scale did the taped joints hold together best? Why do you think this was so?

◆ How is the "feel" of the large cantilever different from that of the small cantilever?

◆ What is it about the small and large cantilevers that create a different reaction or impression in the viewer?

After a good deal of discussion, a simple demonstration is helpful. Tape four skewers together with overlapped joints to form a piece about 24 inches long. Tape four garden poles together with overlapped joints to form a piece about 14 feet long. Now try to hold these pieces out rigidly from the end of a table. The skewers will stay fairly rigid. The garden poles will droop significantly. Ask your students to connect this to what they saw in their structures.

What's Going On

Building on two scales gives clear examples of how some relationships of physical properties change with scale and others remain the same. On both scales, triangular elements were the most stable. However, structures seem less rigid and more ready to twist on the larger scale.

The proportions of the skewer and the garden poles were the same. (This means that if the skewers are 200 times as long as they are thick, then the garden poles are also 200 times as long as they are thick.) The linear dimensions of the garden poles are 6 times the size of the corresponding linear dimensions of the skewers. This means garden pole areas are 36 (6^2) times larger than the skewer areas. Garden pole volume is 216 (6^3) times larger than the skewer volume. The physical consequences of this are dramatic. Strength depends on cross-sectional area. This means garden poles are 36 times as strong as skewers. However, weight depends on volume. Garden poles weigh 216 times as much as skewers. Garden pole structures have to support greater weight for their strength and are therefore more floppy.

This effect is exaggerated in cantilevers. Since cantilevers are built out from a support, the distance of the weight from the support acting on the structure becomes a dominant factor. For the garden pole cantilevers, not only are they heavier than their skewer counterparts, but their center-of-mass is farther out from the support, creating proportionally greater torque. This adds to the bending that can be seen in these structures.

Extensions

◆ **Tie-in to the *Straw and Pins—Building Out* activity:** This activity can be scaled up significantly by using plastic golf tubes and nails or wire. Plastic golf tubes are sold in some shops that carry golf supplies. They have $1\frac{1}{2}$-inch diameters and are as long as the shaft of a golf club. A set of these is rather expensive, so if you use them, you will probably just get one set for the class. To get repeated use, try putting holes in the tubes with a hole punch and joining the tubes with wire. This activity can be scaled down by using cocktail straws and the smallest pins available at a sewing store. The scale change is not large but the effects are still noticeable.

◆ **Tie-in to the *Clay Bridges* activity:** This activity can lend itself to illustrating the effects of scale on structure simply by trying to build bridges with different amounts of clay. Can you build a bridge twice as long with twice as much clay? How much clay do you need to build a bridge half as long? Have your students test their predictions. (See the *Clay Beams and Columns* activity for more on scaling with clay.)

◆ **Tie-in to the *Paper Bridges* activity:** Experimentation with larger sheets of heavier paper or smaller sheets of onionskin paper can lead to scale comparisons here. The findings here are much more qualitative since scaling, especially for paper thickness, is much less controlled.

◆ **Tie-in to the *Building with Newspaper* activities:** See *Scaled Newspaper Structures* in this section for scale work with newspapers.

Scaled Newspaper Structures

TIME

- Three sessions of 60–90 minutes

PREPARATION

- Cut newspaper to scale (see inset).
- Set out the materials.

GROUPING

- Two to four students

MATERIALS
(per group)

- Several Sunday newspapers
- One-half roll of masking tape
- Ruler
- Optional: glue

TEACHER TIPS

- Have a central location for supplies for when the students need more.
- Pass out tape one yard at a time. Have the group designate one of its members as the "tape getter" for when they need more tape.
- If your students have no experience working with newspaper, they will need a chance to experiment and see what they can do to make it stronger. Since newspaper is a very weak material, it must be manipulated (folded, rolled, layered, twisted) in order to gain strength.

Context

Students have the opportunity to investigate building structures on different scales with an inherently flimsy material. First, they can explore the relationship between the material and the shape, stability, and strength of the structure they build with it on a desktop scale. They can then observe how these relationships shift with a change in scale by building on a smaller and on a larger scale. Since newspaper is not generally thought of as a decorative element, its use helps the learner focus on the aesthetic and mechanical elements of the structure itself.

What It Is

Students build newspaper structures on three different scales: first, a medium scale of $1\frac{1}{2}$ feet; then, a smaller scale of 8 inches; and finally, a larger scale of 6 feet.

Begin the activity with a class brainstorm about different human-made or natural structures that have an outside/inside, or an exterior/interior. Share pictures from books. In addition to the mechanics of the structure, we want students to think about the feel of the structure and its aesthetics. Then ask the students to build a structure:

◆ with an inside and an outside (interior and exterior space)

◆ using the medium-sized rectangles of paper (see inset below)

◆ with at least one dimension being exactly $1\frac{1}{2}$ feet (either height, width, or depth)

◆ that has strength.

Work with the students to come up with some parameters for the structure, such as 50–100 pieces of paper per group or 3 yards of tape per group.

After agreeing on the parameters, students can plan their designs by drawing or discussion, or they can dive right into the materials and begin building.

In subsequent sessions, use the same approach to build a small structure, using the small-structure-sized paper, with the stipulation that one dimension be 8 inches. In the final session, have the students build large structures, using the large-structure-sized paper, with the stipulation that one dimension be 6 feet.

Preparation of Materials

Large Structures—6-foot scale—use several Sunday newspapers of full sheets of newspaper.

Medium Structures—$1\frac{1}{2}$-foot scale—take several Sunday newspapers. Cut individual pages into three lengths and then cut each length into three rectangles. You will get nine pieces from the original page.

Small Structures—8-inch scale—take several medium-structure newspaper rectangles, cut each rectangle into three lengths and then cut each length into three rectangles. Each medium-structure rectangle will yield nine small-structure rectangles.

Discussing Results

To help the students reflect on the activity and what they have learned, after each building session have them write and/or draw about what worked and what didn't, what changes they made as they went along, what surprised them, and what they think they learned.

Ask the students what they have discovered about the newspaper as well as the building process. Did they plan their work? Was it easy to follow the plan or not? What changes did they make? When? Why?

When the students build on small or large scales, ask them to compare building on the different scales. What was easier or harder on each scale? On which scale did the material seem stronger? On which was it weaker? What did they have to do to compensate on the weaker scale?

In addition, talk about the feel of their structures on different scales. Think about what it would be like to be a scaled-down person and go into each of the structures. Try going into the large-scale structure.

What's Going On

Students will see the same material acting in different ways at different scales. For example, at a small scale the newspaper seems to be strong but hard to work with. At a larger scale, the paper is more obviously flimsy. This is because of the difference in the ratio of area to volume. Strength depends on area. Weight depends on volume. As you scale up, the volume increases more than the area. Therefore, the weight increases more than the strength and the newspaper is unable to support its own weight. Also coming into play are the effects of torque (the distance of weight from a pivot point). Tubes made from a full sheet of newspaper are more likely to twist and collapse than tubes made from a smaller rectangle. With the longer tube, more of the weight is far from the end where the tube is attached and can pivot.

Extensions

- Build structures out of various materials (milk cartons, corks, paper towel tubes) with different dimensions.

- On one scale, investigate what happens when you treat the same material differently. Have the students build structures of varying scale out of newspaper rolled in tubes; crumpled in balls; folded in sheets, etc.

Clay Beams and Columns

TIME

◆ 30–60 minutes

PREPARATION

◆ Prepare clay beam molds (see inset).
◆ Set out materials.

GROUPING

◆ Pairs or table groups for demonstration

MATERIALS
(per pair or group)

◆ 2 pounds or more of plasticene (modeling clay)
◆ Butter knife, steel rule, wire, or dental floss for cutting clay
◆ Ruler
◆ Paper to work on

TEACHER TIPS

◆ Plasticene is an oil-based clay. It leaves an oily residue on surfaces. Work on paper and/or be prepared to clean desks with soap or other grease remover.
◆ If you have students do this in pairs, try setting it up as a center where a subgroup of your class can work while the rest works on something else. This saves on the number of beam molds that you need to make and the total amount of plasticene that you need.

Context

The central idea of this activity is that when you scale up proportionally (i.e., keep things the same shape but change the size) weight increases faster than strength. These beams afford a dramatic demonstration of that fact, and the activity therefore works quite well as a demonstration. It can also extend into inquiry, by using the proportional clay beams formed in the beam molds as the raw material for investigation.

What It Is

Before beginning this activity, you must build at least one set of beam molds as described in the inset.

Building a Set of Beam Molds

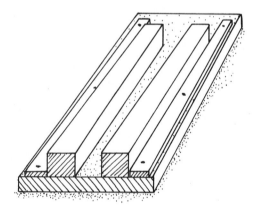

Beam molds can be built with scrap lumber and wooden moldings, or with materials purchased from a lumber yard. For a set, you will build one mold for $\frac{1}{4}$-inch-by-$\frac{1}{4}$-inch cross-section beams (small mold) and one mold for 1-inch-by-1-inch cross-section beams (large mold). Materials for one set are listed below.

- Bases: 3-foot 1-by-6 pine or fir or $\frac{3}{4}$-inch plywood

- Stops: 6-foot $\frac{1}{4}$-inch-by-$\frac{1}{2}$-inch screen mold or $\frac{1}{4}$-inch plywood

- Forms for large beams: 4-foot 1-inch-by-1-inch pine square molding

- Forms for small beams: 2-foot $\frac{1}{4}$-inch-by-$\frac{1}{2}$-inch screen molding

- 8–12 finishing nails ($\frac{3}{4}$-inch long)

To make the bases for the two molds, cut the 3-foot 1-by-6 into two pieces, one 26 inches long and the other 10 inches long.

To make the guides to hold your removable forms in place while molding the clay, cut the $\frac{1}{4}$-inch "stop" material into two 26-inch pieces and two 10-inch pieces.

To make the removable molds for the large beams, cut the 1-inch-by-1-inch pine square molding into two 20-inch pieces and save the leftover piece for a spacer to use while you are nailing in the stops.

To make the removable molds for the small beams, cut the $\frac{1}{4}$-inch-by-$\frac{1}{2}$-inch screen molding into two 10-inch pieces and save the leftover piece for a spacer to use while you are nailing in the stops.

Constructing the large beam mold: First, nail one 20-inch piece of "stop" material along one edge of the 1-by-6 base using 3 or 4 nails. Then, set up the mold as shown in the illustration. Set your leftover piece of 1-inch-by-1-inch stop in the center as a spacer. Then nail the other spacer in place using 3 or 4 nails.

Constructing the small beam mold: The only difference in making the small beam mold is that you turn the $\frac{1}{4}$-inch-by-$\frac{1}{2}$-inch leftover piece on edge when you use it as a spacer and you don't use quite as many nails.

You are now ready to make clay beams using these molds.

To make clay beams, start by working the clay to make it pliable. To make the large beam, set the 1-by-1 removable mold piece against the stops and stuff clay into the mold as tightly as possible. Using your knife or metal rule, smooth down the top of the clay so that it is even with the top edges of the mold. Then, keeping the removable mold and clay together, turn over the mold and reset it between the stops. You will see some unfilled holes in the bottom of the clay beam. Stuff more clay in to fill these holes and smooth down the clay so that it is even with the top edges of the mold again. Lift the moveable mold and clay and pull apart the wood pieces. You now have a 1-inch-by-1-inch clay beam. You can trim it to the length that you want for various purposes.

Making the small beam is very similar to making the large one. The only thing to look out for is that the screen mold has one edge that is rounded rather than square. That edge should be set against the stop in order to get the proper $\frac{1}{4}$-inch-by-$\frac{1}{4}$-inch beam.

Clay Beams and Columns

To do the demonstration with the beams you make the big beam four times as long as the small beam. This maintains the constant linear proportion of 4 to 1. You want to choose lengths that clearly show the difference in rigidity of the two scales. We usually make the small beam about 6 cm long and the large beam about 24 cm long. The length that works best for you will depend on the consistency of your clay, how much it has been handled, and the temperature of the room where you are working. Experiment and see what works best.

Make or have your students make enough beams so that each group of no more than eight students can have a large one and a small one. Ask your students to compare the two beams.

- Have them compare length, width, and depth. They should see for themselves that each of these is four times as large on the big beam.

- Have them try to stand each piece as a column. Ask them which is easier to get to stand. Both may stand a while, but the big one will bend over much sooner.

- Have them hold the clay beam by the end and try to lift each. The big beam droops immediately, whereas the small one is relatively stiff.

This demonstration shows in a very concrete manner the fact that when you scale up proportionally (i.e., keep things the same shape but change the size), weight increases faster than strength.

To initiate a more open-ended activity with these materials, use the clay beam molds to make raw materials for building at different scales and try some of these suggestions.

- Make a lot of clay beams on both the small and large scales. Use them as basic building materials to build structures of the students' choice. In the first session, try building on each scale without mixing pieces. Ask your students to compare the structures that they built out of big pieces with the structures that they built out of small pieces. How were the structures similar? How were they different? Were there things that you could do at one scale but not at the other? In other sessions, students can try mixing large- and small-scale beams. How did they use each of the sizes in their mixed structure?

- Build *trees*. Cut a small beam about 3 cm long and use it as a *tree trunk*. Add clay to it to fill out the top of the tree. Cut a large beam four times as long to make a bigger tree. Add clay to fill out its top of this bigger tree. Ask your students to compare the small tree and the large tree. Can the two trees have the same proportions? How does the scale change force you to make a differ-ent-looking tree?

- Build *animals*. Cut four small beams about 3 cm long and use them as *animal legs*. Add clay to make the body, head, tail, and other parts of the animal. Cut four large beams each four times as long as the small beams. Again, add clay to make a body, head, tail, and other parts of the bigger animal. Ask your students to compare the small animal and the large animal. What do their animals look like (e.g., a dog, a mouse, an elephant)? Can the two animals have the same proportions? How does the scale change force you to make a different animal?

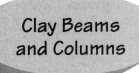

Clay Beams and Columns

Discussing Results

If the more open-ended activity is done in a center as suggested above, it is best to have students write about their experience. Have them respond to some of the questions above.

For the demonstration part of this activity, ask your students what they observed when looking at the large and small clay beams. Which was stiffer? Which was stronger? Which bent over the fastest? Ask them why they think the clay beams behaved differently on the two scales.

Try to connect this work to work they may have done in the *Mathematics of Scale* section. Ask them how much more clay there is in the big beam (64 times as much). Ask them how much more the big beam weighs (64 times the weight). Ask them how much greater the area of the base (or cross-sectional area) is for the big beam (16 times the area). Ask them how much stronger the big beam is (16 times as strong). Then ask if this helps explain why things were different on the two scales.

What's Going On

The linear dimensions of the big clay beams are 4 times that of the small clay beams. They are 4 times as long, 4 times as wide, and 4 times as thick. This means that the volume of the big beam is $4 \times 4 \times 4 = 64$ times the volume of the small beam. This means 64 times as much clay which is 64 times as heavy.

The area of the big beam is $4 \times 4 = 16$ times the area of the small beam. Since strength depends on the area of the cross-section of a beam or column, the big clay beam is 16 times as strong as the little clay beam. The increase of the volume (64 times) of the big clay beam over the little clay beam is 4 times as great as the increase of area (16 times). This means that the increase in weight of the big beam over the little beam is 4 times as great as the increase in strength. The big beam cannot easily support its own weight and collapses and bends much more than the small beam.

Extensions

◆ When building clay trees and animals with large versus small clay trunks or legs, your students find a number of differences. Have them bring in pictures of actual large and small trees and animals to look for similar differences.

Water Drop Pennies

TIME

◆ 45 minutes

PREPARATION

◆ Set out materials.

GROUPING

◆ Pairs

MATERIALS
(per pair)

◆ Eyedropper or straws cut into 3-inch pieces to use as droppers
◆ Penny
◆ Hand lens
◆ Small container of water
◆ Stack of paper towels for mopping up spills
◆ Paper for recording results

Context

Students will be able to observe the effects of surface tension of water. Water surface tension allows students to pile up a lot more drops on the penny than they would have thought possible. The water forms a large "bubble" on the penny. The weight of the water (or gravity pulling at the water) would tend to make the water run off the penny, but surface tension works to hold the "bubble" together and to prevent the water from running off the penny. In essence, the surface of the water supports some of the weight of the water contained within that surface.

The interplay of surface tension of water and the weight of water or the objects on the surface is a quick way to observe some of the effects of changing scale. We explore this interplay in the *Water Domes, Exploring Water Drops,* and *Floating Pins and Paper Clips* activities that follow. *Water Drop Pennies* is a nice introduction to the surprising nature of surface tension and an important precursor to the aforementioned activities.

What It Is

Put some paper towels on the table. Have the students practice filling the eye-dropper with water and carefully squeezing out one drop at a time into the container. Ask them to count the drops during this process so that they can get used to the rate at which the drops fall.

Ask them to put the penny on the paper towel in front of them. Have them take the penny and squeeze two drops onto it. One student can drop the water and the other can count the number of drops. You may set some standards of procedure, such as the height from which the water should be dropped. Ask them to observe the relationship between the size of the water drop and the diameter of the penny.

Next, have them estimate how many drops of water a penny will hold before the water spills over onto the towel. Ask them to write down their predictions in pen or crayon. Have the students begin to add one drop of water at a time to the penny, counting and recording as they proceed. When the penny overflows, ask them to dry it with a paper towel and continue.

This time, as they near the expected limit of drops, ask them to take the hand lens and examine the penny. They will be able to see that the water forms a "bubble"—or dome—on top of the penny. Have them draw pictures of the shape of the water dome as part of their record of this activity.

Discussing Results

As a class, record the student observations about the activity on the blackboard. Compare the results of the activity with the student predictions. Ask questions such as:

◆ How many students had an estimate close to the actual number of drops held by the penny?

◆ How many students estimated lower? higher?

◆ Who was surprised by the results?

◆ What is the average number of drops a penny will hold?

◆ What variables did you observe? Would small differences, such as a change in the size of the eyedropper opening, or a penny surrounded by a higher ridge, make a large or a small difference?

◆ What about the shape of the water drop? When you double the volume (i.e., double the number of drops), do the height and diameter also double?

Introduce the concept of surface tension, which allows a container to hold more than seems possible.

What's Going On

Water molecules align on the water surface to form a skinlike surface. This property of water is called *surface tension*. The surface of the water on the penny acts like a little sack holding many drops. The strength of the surface tension depends on the perimeter, a linear dimension.

Extensions

◆ Flip the coin over and repeat the procedure. Compare the result.

◆ Use different-sized coins. Graph the coin's diameter versus the number of drops the coin holds to examine how volume increases as linear dimensions increase. A coin with double the diameter of a penny (e.g., a 50-cent piece) has 4 times the area. If the water dome on top of the coin had the same shape (i.e., proportions) as that on top of the smaller coin, you would expect it to be twice as high as the water dome on the smaller coin. In that case, the double diameter coin would hold 8 (2^3) times as many drops. However, this is not the case. The surface tension depends on surface area, whereas the weight supported depends on volume. The increase in surface strength is not great enough to support 8 times the weight. The water dome formed will, therefore, be less than twice as tall as with the smaller coin, and the dome will hold a good deal less than 8 times as many drops.

◆ Dip the end of a toothpick into some dishwashing liquid. Touch the end of the toothpick to the water on the penny. The water "bubble" will collapse because soap greatly reduces the surface tension of water.

Water Domes

TIME

◆ 45 minutes

PREPARATION

◆ Set out materials.

GROUPING

◆ Pairs

MATERIALS
(per pair)

◆ Eyedropper
◆ Two or more container lids of the same material and design but different sizes (e.g., a metal alcohol bottle lid and a metal mayonnaise bottle lid)
◆ Small containers of water
◆ Paper towels
◆ Paper for recording results

TEACHER TIPS

◆ Have your students collect and bring container lids from home.

Context

This activity should follow *Water Drop Pennies* and may be done at the same session if you have time. It is a clear-cut example of the effect of changing the scale on the shape of a structure.

What It Is

Put some paper towels on the table. Have the students fill each container lid with as much water as they can. Have the lids sitting side by side so that the differences are easy to observe. They will be able to see that the water forms a different-shaped dome on each of the lids. Have them draw pictures of the shapes of the water domes as part of their record of this activity.

Discussing Results

As a class, record the student observations about the activity on the chalkboard. Compare the results of the activity for different-sized lids. Ask questions such as:

◆ Which lids held rounder domes and which lids held flatter domes?

◆ Who was surprised by the results? Why?

◆ What variables did you observe? Does the material from which the lid is made or the way the edge of the lid is constructed make a difference?

Ask students to hypothesize an explanation for the differences that they observe.

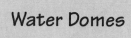

Water Domes

What's Going On

The surface of the water in the lid acts like a little sack holding the water that sticks over the top of the edge. The strength of the surface tension depends on the perimeter length. The weight of the water pulls it down, tending to make it run over the edge. The weight of this water depends on the volume of the dome. The weight of the water and the strength of the surface tension are two competing forces.

When you have a smaller lid, the perimeter is long for the volume present, the surface tension force can support proportionally more water, and the dome is rounder. When you have a larger lid, the perimeter is short for the volume present, the surface tension force can support proportionally less water, and the dome is flatter than on a smaller lid. For example, a lid with 4 times the diameter has 16 (4^2) times the area. If the water dome on top of the lid had the same shape (i.e., proportion) as that on top of the smaller lid, you would expect it to be 4 times as high as the water dome on the smaller lid. In that case, the larger diameter lid would hold 64 (4^3) times as much water. However, this is not the case. The increase in surface strength is not great enough to support 64 times the weight. The water dome formed will, therefore, be less than 4 times as tall as that of the smaller lid, and the dome will hold a good deal less than 64 times as much water.

Extensions

♦ Dip the end of a toothpick into some dishwashing liquid. Touch the end of the toothpick to the water in the lid. The water dome will collapse because soap greatly reduces the surface tension of water.

Exploring Water Drops

TIME

- ◆ 30–40 minutes

PREPARATION

- ◆ Set out materials.
- ◆ Tape down a sheet (about 12 inches) of wax paper for each student.

GROUPING

- ◆ Individuals or pairs

MATERIALS

(per individual or pair)

- ◆ Eyedropper
- ◆ Container with water (which can be shared at tables)
- ◆ Sheet of wax paper
- ◆ Tape (which can be shared at tables)
- ◆ Paper towels

TEACHER TIPS

- ◆ Be ready with paper towels.
- ◆ Black construction paper placed under the wax paper makes viewing the water drops easier.

Context

This activity follows *Water Drop Pennies* and *Water Domes* and is an early activity to show the effect of scale on structure. It provides one of several examples of how size affects the shapes formed by surface tension.

What It Is

Have the students practice using the eyedropper for a few minutes by dropping water back into the water container on the table. Ask them to count out a few drops so that they become familiar with the rate of the dropper. When they are ready, take them through the following series of steps:

- ◆ Ask them to take the eyedropper and start to make drops on the sheet of wax paper in front of them. Give them a good deal of time to explore without your direction. Have them write and draw their discoveries.

◆ Ask them to see how many different types of water drops they can make. Show them how to lift one end of the wax paper to make the drops move. Ask them to make big drops and small ones. When their sheets of wax paper become saturated, tell them to carefully pick up the paper and pour the water back into the container. Have them draw side views of the big and small drops.

◆ Ask the students to make a row of water drops all of the same size.

◆ Ask them to put the drops as close together as they can, without letting the drops touch one another. Ask them to pick up one end of the wax paper so that the drops gently roll into one another. What happens?

◆ What happens when you take a pencil and try to gently pull at the water drop?

◆ Try to drop the water from high up. What happens when it lands?

◆ Ask students to make very small drops and very large drops.

Discussing Results

Record the students' observations about the activity on a piece of chart paper or the chalkboard. Have them share the discoveries that they recorded. Have them talk about the different shapes they found in the big and small drops. Ask questions along the following lines:

◆ What did the water drops look like?

◆ What happened when two or more drops came together?

◆ How did the water drops move across the wax paper?

◆ What surprised you about water drops?

◆ What did you learn about water drops?

◆ What other things would you like to investigate about water drops?

What's Going On

A key observation here is the difference in the shape of small and large drops on a surface like wax paper. As the drops grow, they get flatter and flatter: a pure scaling phenomenon. Surface tension, which is dependent on the perimeter length, pulls the drops into a spherical shape. Gravity—in this case the weight of the water being pulled toward earth—which depends on volume, pulls the water downward into a flat shape.

For small drops, the weight of the water in the drop is small compared to the surface tension, so the drop retains a spherical shape. As you add more water, the volume grows faster than the perimeter length, and the weight becomes more and more dominant. Thus, you have flattened drops (see the overview of *The Physics and Engineering of Structure* for more on this battle between weight and strength).

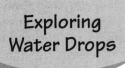

Exploring Water Drops

Extensions

◆ Try repeating the procedure using different liquids such as oil, milk, vinegar. Are the effects the same?

◆ Variations using water or other liquids include

1. dropping the water onto different surfaces (newspaper, tin foil, tabletops)

2. using different droppers, a straw, an empty pen case. Does the size of the dropper's hole make a difference in the size of the drop?

3. using several different liquids and looking at the drops from the edge of the table. Are all of the drops the same shape? Can you tell from the shape which liquid has been used?

Floating Pins and Paper Clips

TIME

♦ 45 minutes

PREPARATION

♦ Set out materials.

GROUPING

♦ Individuals or pairs

MATERIALS
(per person or pair)

♦ A wide container (e.g., pie plate or wide-mouth plastic cup)
♦ Small paper clip bent into an L-shape to use as a hook
♦ Small and large paper clips, one of each size for every two students
♦ Small and large straight pins or needles, one of each size for every two students
♦ Paper towels
♦ Optional: Get different gauges (thicknesses) of wire from a hardware store. Choose a base length and gauge of wire and then get sizes that are twice as big, three times, four times, five times, etc. Using proportionately larger and smaller gauges of wire will show very clearly how the change in scale affects the experiment. Choose a base size that will allow two or three of the different gauge wires to "float."

TEACHER TIPS

♦ Water containers must be free of soap residue.
♦ Make sure objects span a large enough range to see the change in floating behavior. Test them first.
♦ Rubbing pins and clips in one's hands "greases" them and keeps them drier.

Context

The objects that students try to "float" in this activity are all denser than water: they therefore can't float in the conventional sense. However, if the objects are small enough and set very carefully on the surface of the water, the water's surface tension keeps them from sinking, making them appear to "float."

What It Is

Give each student a wide container filled almost to the top with water. Ask the students to find out which, if any, of the pins, paper clips, or wire will "float" on the water surface. It's important to have them start with the small paper clips, as almost all of them will find success with this size.

♦ The students should use the small paper clip bent into an L-shape to help lower the clip into the cup.

◆ Each time they have to try again, they should dry off and "waterproof" their pins or clips by rubbing them with their hands.

◆ After they try the small paper clip, they should move on to other sizes.

◆ Be ready with paper towels!

Different students find success with this activity at different rates. The small paper clips must be lowered gently into the water so that the surface tension is not broken. When you see that a student has successfully gotten the small paper clip to "float," ask him or her to see if the large paper clip will "float" (it won't very easily). After many attempts, students will start to speculate as to why the large paper clips sink. They should move on to different-sized objects. Make sure all students see that any clip put in the water end-first will sink.

Have the students experiment with wood, plastic paper clips, and other objects that float normally. It is useful for them to experience the difference between objects that float normally, because they are less dense than water, and objects that ride on the water surface supported by surface tension.

When the activity is over, go around to the different tables with a bucket and have the students empty their water containers into the bucket. This avoids the potential disasters which might result from sending thirty students with water containers off to the classroom sink.

Discussing Results

Compile a class chart by asking the students which pins, paper clips, or wires floated and which did not. Some helpful questions to ask include:

◆ What did you observe during the activity?

◆ Who was able to float which object?

◆ Which objects did not float? Why not?

◆ How were "floating" metal clips different from wood or plastic floaters?

Discuss the idea of surface tension.

What's Going On

Students will find that the larger objects always sink, whereas the smaller ones can be made to "float" on the surface. Surface tension will provide enough upward force on the small object to balance the weight (downward pull of gravity). Buoyancy will also help with the upward force, but it is not enough with these objects, which are denser than water.

The upward force depends on the perimeter of the object. The weight depends on the volume. If you scale up the floating object by a factor of two, the linear dimensions increase by two: it is twice as long, twice as wide, and twice as thick—the perimeter has doubled. But its volume, and hence weight, is eight times as great. The surface tension of the water cannot support the volume/weight, and the big paper clip sinks.

Extensions

◆ See if the containers of water can hold two small paper clips.

◆ Point the end of a toothpick into some liquid detergent. Then point the tooth-pick into the water on which a small object is floating. The object will sink to the bottom because soap greatly reduces the surface tension of water.

Beyond This Book—Scale and Structure in the World

In this book, we have looked at how a change of scale affects the relationship between the weight and strength of objects and how this in turn affects structure and proportion. You can understand these changes with scale by studying the different way linear dimensions, areas, and volumes change with scale changes and by recognizing how weight and strength relate to these quantities. There are many other physical properties that depend on either length, area, or volume. We can extend our look at differences that depend on scale by looking at some of these properties.

Chemical reactions, for instance, depend on the amount of surface contact between reactants. When you eat, food reacts with digestive fluids in your stomach. A big lump of food in your stomach would take a long time to digest. But you don't swallow food whole. Chewing food increases its exposed surface, allowing for fast digestion. Even something as simple as dissolving sugar shows the same effect. A sugar cube takes quite a while to dissolve. The same amount of granulated sugar dissolves rapidly. The exact same analysis that explains these everyday phenomena can be applied to less familiar processes. Take the chemical reaction between oxygen and gasoline, for instance. A puddle of gasoline will burn for many minutes, slowly releasing its energy. If you atomize it, spraying it into the air, and ignite it, you will actually get an explosion, releasing all of the energy at once. Increasing the surface area of the gasoline exposed to the air speeds the burning reaction. This is what the carburetor in your car does.

Heat flow is another phenomenon that depends on surface area. The greater the surface area for a particular volume, the greater the rate of heat flow. You can see your pet cat taking advantage of this fact. On a cold day, your cat curls up to reduce its exposed surface area, reducing its rate of heat loss. On a hot day, your cat will stretch out to increase its exposed surface area and hence increase its rate of heat flow. This keeps the cat cooler.

You use this principle in cooking as well. If you want to boil your potato quickly you cut it into smaller pieces. This allows the heat to flow into the potato faster, thus cooking it faster.

The same analysis that explains these everyday experiences can be applied to less familiar phenomena. For instance, small electronic transformers have simple box casings with wire coils inside. Waste heat produced by the wire flows across the surface of the casing. Heat production depends on volume. Since volume grows faster than area, large transformers must be specially designed to keep from melting from the proportionately greater amount of heat. The solution is to increase the surface area by adding metal "fins" to the casings.

These heat flow considerations are important in warm-blooded animals as well. Small animals have a lot of surface area (skin) compared to their volume (weight) when compared with larger animals. They produce little heat because of their low weight. What is produced is quickly lost through the relatively small surface area of their skin. Consequently, these animals have to consume great quantities of food to replace the lost heat. It seems to us that small birds do almost nothing but eat all day. They must eat to get the energy needed to replace the lost heat that they need to stay alive.

Speaking of eating, absorption of nutrients and elimination of waste is also affected by scale relationships. In small protozoa, you find that a particle of food is engulfed in a small vacuole, which floats free in the cytoplasm during the digestive process. Once digestion is completed, this food vacuole moves to the surface membrane and opens to the exterior, thus expelling the undigested wastes. In somewhat larger, multicellular forms, there is usually an alimentary canal with a mouth at one end and an anus at the other. However, the amount of nutrients needed and waste produced depends on the volume. The rate of absorption of nutrients and elimination of waste depends on the amount of gut surface area. Therefore, large creatures need different designs than small ones. Elaborate folds and creases are present in animal intestines to increase the surface area.

Animals must also breathe. They must supply oxygen to all of their cells and eliminate carbon dioxide. This is not difficult for small creatures with only tens or even hundreds of cells. But since the number of cells grows with volume and the surface area for absorbing oxygen grows more slowly, creative designs of multiple branching lungs are needed to increase surface area to supply enough oxygen for all the cells in larger animals. Also, elaborate, branching circulatory systems with intricate capillary systems are needed to transport the oxygen to the cells. Insects, which are much smaller, do not transport oxygen with their blood. Instead, air-filled tubes carry oxygen directly to muscles and organs, where it can diffuse directly to nearby cells. This mechanism directly limits the size of insects.

Large plants face similar needs. Elaborate branching root systems culminating in many minute root hairs increase the surface area for absorption of water and nutrients. Large trees break into complex branches with a lot of leaf area to increase the absorption of solar energy and the exchange of oxygen and carbon dioxide.

Another everyday phenomenon that can be examined is the fact that ants can walk on walls and ceilings, while we cannot. The cohesive force that holds the ant to the wall depends on the length of the perimeter of the foot. The force pulling on them is their weight, which depends on volume. Since volume decreases much faster than length, the cohesive force plays a much bigger role for the ant than for us. (For more about the world of the ant, see the inset.)

Examples of structures dependent on their scale are all around us. Once you start to think this way, you see them everywhere. The experience of working with structure and scale gives you and your students a powerful new lens through which to view and appreciate the world.

Ants and Us

We differ from ants in many ways, but size is certainly an important difference, important especially because of its consequences. For instance, ants could not use fire, for even the smallest possible stable campfire flame is larger than an ant. Keeping a wood fire burning would be quite beyond their capacity, because ants are too small to get near enough to add fuel (which, in any event, they would be unable to carry). Ants cannot use tools. A miniature hammer has too little kinetic energy to drive even a miniature nail. Spears, arrows, and clubs, which depend on a suitable ratio of kinetic energy to a characteristic surface area to do their work, would be inefficient at ant size. Ant-sized books would be impossible to manufacture, or even to open, because the thin pages would stick together owing to intermolecular forces that are relatively powerful at that scale. In any event, reading would likely have few charms for ants because, with their small size, they have very few brain cells. Of course, ants have enough neurons to do all of the remarkable things that ants normally do, but we modestly presume that, in order for an animal to appreciate the joys of literature, it needs to be at least the size of a human being.

And finally, to emphasize our great superiority to ants, they cannot wash themselves in water. The water droplets of a shower stream come in a certain minimum size. Droplets of even this minimum size would strike an ant like heavy missiles. Even if an ant tried to take a bath in a single drop, surface tension would interfere because the skin of the ant's body is water-repellent. If the ant did somehow manage to get into a drop of water, surface tension would make it difficult to get out again. (It is not uncommon to see a fly struggling to extricate a leg from a drop of liquid on a flat surface.) The answer for the ant is to dry-clean itself by rubbing particles of dry substances over its body and then scraping the particles off.

There are, however, certain advantages to being an ant. An ant can lift ten times its own weight. It can fall large distances without injury. At certain times in the lives of some ants, they fly by using an awkward mechanism that would never serve to get a human being off of the ground.
—Fritz W. Went, *On Size and Life*

Appendix A

Glossary

Area: The total surface of anything. It is measured in square units.

Beam: A horizontal building element.

Cantilever: A projecting beam or other structure supported only at one end.

Center-of-Mass: The balance point of any object. The weight of an object can be treated as if it were all concentrated at this point.

Column: A vertical building element.

Compression: The state of a material made more compact by pressure.

Dimension: Any measurable extent as length, breadth, thickness, etc.

Equilibrium, Linear: The balance of forces in a nonaccelerating structure.

Equilibrium, Rotational: The balance of torques in a structure that is not rotating.

Forces: Pushes or pulls on objects.

Fulcrum: The support or point of support on which a lever turns in raising or moving something.

Gravity: On earth, the force that tends to draw all bodies in the earth's sphere toward the center of the earth. In general, an attractive force between any two masses.

Joint: A place or part where two things or parts are joined.

Length: Any linear dimension, including perimeters, diameters, and circumferences.

Linear Dimension: Any length, including perimeters, diameters, and circumferences.

Load, Dead: The weight of a structure itself.

Load, Live: The weight of anything on a structure.

Plumb Line: Line used to establish a true vertical.

Scale: 1) The relative size being considered, as in microscopic, human, or cosmic scale; 2) the ratio between dimensions of a representation and those of the object.

Shear Force: The force that causes two contacting parts or layers to slide upon each other, moving apart in opposite directions parallel to the plane of their contact.

Stabiles: An abstract sculpture with no moving parts, using balance as an aesthetic element.

Stability: The capacity of an object to return to equilibrium or to its original position after having been displaced.

Structure: The arrangement or interrelation of all the parts of a whole.

Surface Tension: The tendency of the surface of a liquid to contract in area and thus behave like a stretched rubber membrane.

Symmetry: Similarity of form or arrangement on either side of a dividing line or plane; correspondence of opposite parts in size, shape, and position.

Tension: A stress on a material produced by the pull of forces tending to cause extension.

Torque: The combination of force and distance from a pivot point.

Volume: The amount of space an object occupies.

Appendix B

Resource Guide

BOOKS FOR STUDENTS

Structure: Curriculum and Activities

Architecture and Engineering: An Illustrated Teacher's Manual on Why Buildings Stand Up
Salvadori, Mario, and Michael Temple
New York: New York Academy of Sciences, 1983
Grades: 6+

This companion to Salvadori's **Why Buildings Stand Up** *is written on a fairly complex level, but many of the activities could be adapted for sixth-graders. This resource book will give you plenty of ideas for concepts such as force, equilibrium, tension and compression, beams and columns, and cables and trusses.*

Architecture Is Elementary
Winters, Nathan
Salt Lake City: Gibbs M. Smith Inc., Peregrine Smith Books, 1986
Grades: 6+

This is a concise, coherent presentation of fifty architectural concepts designed to "help the brain interpret what the eye receives." Lessons are grouped at seven developmental levels, written in understandable language, and accompanied by intricate ink drawings depicting a thorough chronology of historic periods and styles.

The Balance Book
Jenkings, Lee
Hayward, Calif.: Activity Resources, 1974
Grades: 2–8

A classic curriculum on balance, this is a teacher's guide for the Elementary Science Study Primary Balance unit. Many of the activities in the Balancing Acts section are derivative of this work.

Building Toothpick Bridges
Pollard, Jeanne
Palo Alto, Calif.: Dale Seymour Publications, 1985
Grades: 5–8

A plan for a class project done in groups involving structure, math, and writing. It is designed for grades 5–8, and would be a good exercise after some exploratory work is done.

Hardhatting in a Geo-World
Fresno, Calif.: AIMS Educational Foundation, 1986
Grades: 3–4

This book contains a number of structure activities which you can incorporate into your scale and structure unit.

I KNOW THAT BUILDING! Discovering Architecture with Activities and Games
D'Alelio, Jan
Washington, D.C.: Preservation Press, 1989
Grades: 4–8

Activities, puzzles, and games.

Investigations, Flea-Sized Surgeons: Surface Area, Volume, and Scale
Berkeley, Calif.: EQUALS, Lawrence Hall of Science, 1994
Grades: 4–8

This book covers material that is very complementary to our work on scale and effects of scale.

Messing Around with Drinking Straw Construction
Zubrowski, Bernie
Boston: Boston Children's Museum, 1981
Grades: 3–8

Students use drinking straws to build their own models of houses, bridges, and towers. They investigate the concept of force and reaction to the stress of gradually increased weight.

Senior Balancing, Teacher's Guide for Elementary Science Study
Newton, Mass.: Educational Development
   Center, 1968
Grades: 4–9

This is an extension of the curriculum of **The Balance Book** (see above).

Structures
An Insights Hands-On Science Module
Newton, Mass.: Educational Development
   Center, 1991
Grades: 5–8

This is a complete structure curriculum designed for upper elementary children. It does a great job of connecting with children's experience outside of school and providing open-ended activities. We recommend it highly.

Structures
Zubrowski, Bernie
White Plains, N.Y.: Cuisenaire, 1993
Grades: 5–8

This book investigates the concept of force and reaction to the stress of gradually increased weight. Students use drinking straws to build their own models of houses, bridges, and towers.

Why Buildings Stand Up
Salvadori, Mario
New York: McGraw-Hill, 1980
Grades: 7+

This book is a veritable tour of the architectural world, from pyramids to bridges, from Gothic cathedrals to skyscrapers, from huts to sports stadiums. Salvadori clearly and simply explains the theory and techniques of structural engineering for the layperson: not only why structures stand up, but why they sometimes fall down. Your students will most likely not be able to read this book in its entirety, but they will enjoy

reading excerpts. A terrific book to stimulate discussion.

Structure: Conceptual Background

The Art of Construction
Salvadori, Mario
New York: Atheneum, 1990
Grades: 5+

By means of models built of commonly available material, the author introduces the basic principles governing the design of buildings, skyscrapers, bridges, and domes and illustrates their applications to architecture by using examples that range from the pyramids to modern high-rise buildings, tents, balloons, and space frames. Many clear drawings help illustrate Salvadori's explanations.

Structures, or Why Things Don't Fall Down
Gordon, J.E.
Jersey City, N.J.: Da Capo, 1978
Grades: 6+

Intermixing humor with solid engineering principles, this book looks at why things, from bridges, dams, and skyscrapers to nightgowns and kangaroos, don't fall down.

What Holds It Together?
Weiss, Harvey
Boston: Little, Brown, 1977
Grades: 4+

This book discusses all methods of "joining" in all human-made structures, from blue jeans to skyscrapers. Weiss covers nails, screws, rivets, gluing, magnets, gravity, tying, melting, and fitting.

What It Feels Like To Be a Building
Wilson, Forrest
Washington, D.C.: Preservation Press,
   1988
Grades: 3+

The design of the book lends itself to large illustrations and little text on every page, yet the text is wonderfully exact, and students will enjoy imagining being a building (e.g., "It feels like squeeze to be an arch, because an arch is all squeezed-push with no pull at all"). Wilson uses human figures (plus some dogs and rams) to show that architecture and people have more in common than one might think. He touches on the most basic qualities of architecture and makes them pleasantly accessible. An excellent way to explain architectural details to children, and the book is sure to stimulate discussion among your students.

Structure: Literature and Connections to Experience

The Architecture of Animals
Forsyth, Adrian
Charlotte, Vt.: Camden House, 1989
Grades: 5+

From spider webs to beaver dams, this children's book shows a great variety of animal constructions. It is full of very nice photos and good accompanying text.

Bridges
Corbett, Scott
New York: MacMillan, 1984
Grades: 4+

This book traces the development of bridge design and construction, focusing on the most interesting and spectacular examples. Included is such information as which bridge is the highest, the longest, the most beautiful, and the most expensive, as well as which bridges have caused some of history's worst tragedies and disasters. More than fifty bridges are featured, from the first attempts at bridge building to the most modern constructions. Pen-and-ink drawings.

The Brooklyn Bridge: They Said It Couldn't Be Built
St. George, Judith
New York: Putnam, 1990
Grades: 5+

The story of how the Brooklyn Bridge was built is fascinating, and this book is the best recitation of that story. Along with the technical engineering information regarding the bridge, St. George tells the remarkable story of the Roebling family, who forged ahead to get the bridge built. Especially interesting are the accounts of the disasters that occurred while the bridge was under construction. Illustrations and historical prints accompany the text.

Building a House
Robbins, Ken
New York: Four Winds, 1984
Grades: 4+

Architects, contractors, electricians, glaziers, and carpenters are among those who work together here as a house is constructed. Photographs and text describe how they use concrete and wood shingles, wire, and fiberglass to do their job. This photo essay introduces readers to a whole process of building a house—from surveying the site to moving in the furniture.

Castle
Macaulay, David
Boston: Houghton Mifflin, 1977
Grades: 4+

Macaulay follows the construction of an imaginary thirteenth-century castle from start to finish. The ideas for the castle are based on the concept, structural process, and physical appearance of several castles built to support the conquest of Wales. As usual, Macaulay includes interesting bits about the lives and needs of the people who lived in these castles.

Cathedral
Macaulay, David
Boston: Houghton Mifflin, 1973
Grades: 5

Similar to **Castle**, this book follows the long, complex construction of an imaginary thirteenth-century cathedral. Clear and simple commentary and Macaulay's usual eye-catching drawings make this an enjoyable, useful book for students and teachers. The glossary is particularly helpful.

From Idea into House
Myller, Rolf
New York: MacMillan, 1974
Grades: 5+

This is a book for anyone who ever wanted to know why it takes so long to build a building. The reader, along with narrator Tia Kummerfeld, witnesses the construction of Tia's family's new house. This is more technical than other similar books, including explanations of purchasing the land, discussions with the architect, and negotiations regarding price. It is also unusual and interesting because the illustrations include the real floor plans and power and plumbing diagrams for the house pictured in the photographs.

How a House Happens
Adkins, Jan
New York: Walker, 1972
Grades: 4+

This unique book takes the reader through the steps of building a house, from choosing the site to planning and finally building. Explanations are brief but to the point and accompanied by entertaining, cartoonlike illustrations.

How Bridges Are Made
Kingston, Jeremy
New York: Facts on File, 1985
Grades: 4+

A good book for children at this level. Beginning with the first bridges, the book traces the history of bridges and their construction. Also included are a chart of "Who Builds Bridges?"; a poster-type spread on the great bridges of the world, with small drawings for identification purposes; and a glossary. Wonderful color photographs.

How They Built the Statue of Liberty
Shapiro, Mary
New York: Random House, 1985
Grades: 3–8

A complete, illustrated book appropriate for children, with a complete history of the statue.

How to Wreck a Building
Horowitz, Elinor Lander
New York: Pantheon, 1982
Grades: 4+

This book lets us join the crowd at the demolition site and watch, step by step, as a seventy-year-old brick school is demolished. The text is written from the point of view of a student who attended the school and who now watches as the building—like everything else that happened there—becomes a memory.

Incredible Constructions and the People Who Built Them
Boring, Mel
New York: Walker, 1984
Grades: 4+

An easy-to-read book about magnificent architectural achievements, such as the Washington Monument, the Panama Canal, and the Hoover Dam. Excellent black-and-white photos and artists' renderings accompany this enlightening text about projects that other people said could not be done. Students will be especially interested in the problems encountered by these builders and how they overcame them. A good book to have in your classroom library.

Pete's House
Sobol, Harriet Langsam
New York: MacMillan, 1978
Grades: 4+

From the day his father takes him to watch the site being cleared until the final visit before moving day, Pete watches the construction of his family's new house. This clear text, accompanied by black-and-white photographs, can help the student understand everything involved in the construction of a house.

Pyramid
Macaulay, David
Boston: Houghton Mifflin, 1975
Grades: 5+

Macaulay discusses the lives of the ancient Egyptians and how and why they built the pyramids. This is a fascinating look at the civilization of an ancient people. It would be a good book to integrate with a social studies unit.

Round Buildings, Square Buildings, and Buildings That Wiggle Like Fish
Isaacson, Philip M.
New York: Knopf, 1988
Grades: 3+

This book communicates the aesthetic aspect of architecture. The author views buildings as beautiful objects and as pieces of social and cultural history. He presents building in terms of how they "feel" to us. The book has a gentle, soft tone and easy language accompanied by excellent color photographs.

This Old New House
McGraw, Shelia
Buffalo, N.Y.: Firefly Books, Ltd.,1989
Grades: 4+

A young boy, Graham, looks on as his parents renovate a rickety old house. The author goes through all the steps, from consulting architects to making up the blueprints and finally to putting on the drywall and finishing touches. The text is enhanced with cartoonlike illustrations, which include colorful cutaways of the house as it is changing.

Unbuilding
Macaulay, David
Boston: Houghton Mifflin, 1987
Grades: 5+

This book is dedicated to "those of us who don't always appreciate things until they are gone," drawing attention to a handsome building while it still stands. Accompanied by beautiful pen-and-ink illustrations, the text tells the fascinating story of the hypothetical step-by-step dismantling of the Empire State Building. Watching this demolition, readers come to realize the precise timing and organization required for such a task.

Underground
Macaulay, David
Boston: Houghton Mifflin, 1976
Grades: 5+

Inventing a site at the intersection of two streets, Macaulay shows the various kinds of foundation constructions that provide support for massive city buildings. He then "opens up" the street and sidewalk to picture the basic city systems: water sewage and drainage, electricity, steam, gas and telephone, subway. The concise text and wonderfully detailed drawings, with illustrations and diagrams, help the reader to

appreciate all the hidden disposal and support networks that allow cities to exist—a fascinating book to read and look at.

Up Goes the Skyscraper
Gibbons, Gail
New York: MacMillan, 1986
Grades: 2+

A beautifully illustrated picture book that may appear at first glance to be too simplistic for your students, but the information in this book is excellent for readers at all levels, and the "comic book" format is appealing to children. This book would be especially useful for ESL students. Easy-to-understand language, aided by color illustrations, conveys the integration of tasks for such a project. It charts the orderly progression of events, from the initial need for a building to its completion.

What Can She Be? An Architect
Goldreich, Ester, and Gloria Goldreich
New York: Lothrop, Lee, and Shepard, 1974
Grades: 4+

Susan Brody is an architect who plans many kinds of buildings. Her work takes her and the reader from her office to a building site, to meetings with clients, and to material suppliers. The book follows her through several projects, including a family home in the city. The text describes how a building is planned and how the architect's instructions are carried out by the construction workers.

Scale

Environmental Geometry
Kirk, Jim
Hayward, Calif.: Activity Resources, 1975
Category: Curriculum and Activities
Grades: K–5

A guide to looking at shapes and sizes found in a child's environment. It includes activities and a very nice section on "strength from shape."

My First Look at Sizes
Oliver, Stephen
New York: Random Books Young
    Readers, 1990

Category: Connections to Experience
Grades: Pre K–6

Crisp, bold, well-labeled photographs present size progressions and comparisons with objects readily found in a child's environment.

My Travels with Gulliver
EDC
Newton, Mass.: Wings for Learning, 1991
Category: Curriculum and Activities
Grades: 2+

This is a math unit that deals with the arithmetic of scaling up and down proportionately using the Gulliver's Travels theme as an organizer. It is a useful precursor to understanding scale and structure.

Powers of Ten: About the Relative Size of Things in the Universe
Morrison, Philip, Phylis Morrison, and the
    office of Charles and Ray Eames
New York: Scientific American Library, 1982
Category: Connections to Experience
Grades: 3+

A journey, in steps of tenfold change, from human scale to the very largest and smallest of scales. Full of photos and loads of information, it is a revealing trip into the world of scale.

Size: The Measure of Things
Laithwaite, Eric
New York: Watts, 1988
Category: Curriculum and Activities
Grades: 4–7

Brief, far-ranging introduction to the significance of size in natural and human-made phenomena. Includes examples, activities, and full-color illustrations.

Two Bad Ants
Van Allsburg, Chris
Boston: Houghton Mifflin, 1988
Category: Literature
Grades: K–4

Well-illustrated children's story showing the world from an ant's point of view.

Books for Teachers

Structure: Curriculum and Activities

City Building Education
Nelson, Doreen
Santa Monica, Calif.: Center for City
    Building Educational Programs, 1982
(Available from the center at 2210
    Wilshire Blvd., Santa Monica, CA
    90403)

This book grew out of a Los Angeles program on city building. It is grounded in a philosophy of integrating the community in which students live with their academic environment. Inventive learning is emphasized, along with critical thinking and discussion. Included is a large section on how to do a city building unit with your students.

Problem Solving in School Science
Johnsey, Robert
London: MacDonald Educational, 1986
(Available from Teachers' Laboratory,
    P.O. Box 6480, Brattleboro, VT
    05301–6480)

An excellent book to use for this entire curriculum. Particularly, it has good activities on strength of materials, structures, and bridges and buildings.

Structure and Forces
Science 5/13
London: MacDonald-Raintree Inc., 1972
(Available through Teachers' Laboratory,
    P.O. Box 6480, Brattleboro, VT
    05301–6480)

An excellent book with great ideas on how to integrate the teaching of structure with many other elements..

Teachers Guide for Structures
Elementary Science Study
Newton, Mass.: Webster Division,
    McGraw-Hill, 1968

A classic with a number of very good, basic activities.

Structure: Conceptual Background

Body, Memory, and Architecture
Bloomer, Kent C., and Charles W. Moore
New Haven, Conn.: Yale University Press, 1977

This book was written to teach the fundamentals of architectural design to first-year students at the Yale School of Architecture. A sometimes difficult book to read, it contains some valuable discussions about what architecture is through the study of the relationships among architecture, the human body, social limitations, and the personal and public implications of architecture. You may gain some ideas for in-depth discussions or research for students.

Life's Devices
Steven Vogel
Princeton, N.J.: Princeton University Press, 1988

Chapter 3 gives an exposition of the effect of scale on animal structure that is more compact and somewhat less technical than **On Size and Life** *(see below).*

The New Science of Strong Materials, or Why You Don't Fall Through the Floor
Gordon, J.E.
Princeton, N.J.: Princeton University Press, 1968

A very readable book focusing on materials themselves. It has some overlap with Gordon's **Structures** *(see below).*

Stone, Clay, Glass: How Building Materials Are Found and Used
Bates, Robert L.
Hillside, N.J.: Enslow Publishers, 1987

This book describes where these vital earth resources are located and how they are found. It also details their use in history by human beings. Resources discussed include stone and concrete, as well as how quartz, sand, and silica are used to make glass.

Structures, or Why Things Don't Fall Down
Gordon, J.E.
Jersey City, N.J.: Da Capo, 1978

A very personal and readable book by an engineer. It includes art, history, and a wide range of ideas. Most of the basic structural concepts can be found here.

Structure: Literature and Connections to Experience

Anatomy of Nature
Feininger, Andreas
New York: Dover, 1979

"How function shapes the form and design of . . . structures throughout the universe." Many photos and some text on structures in nature.*

The Tower and the Bridge: The New Art of Structural Engineering
Billington, David P.
Princeton, N.J.: Princeton University Press, 1985

A lovely book arguing for the artistic nature of structural engineering. It has some great pictures and a history of the development of tower and bridge building.

Scale

On Size and Life
McMahon, Thomas, and Bonner Tyler
New York: Scientific American Books, 1983

This is a bit on the technical side, but it has a lot of good information on the effect of size and scale on living organisms.

On Growth and Form
Thompson, D'Arcy
Cambridge, Mass.: Cambridge University Press, 1917

A classic treatise on the effect of size and materials on the structure of living things.

"On Being the Right Size,"
in **The World of Mathematics,** Vol. 2,
   Newman, J.R., editor
New York: Simon and Schuster, 1956

*A classic and wonderful addition to the set
of examples of the effect of size (i.e., scale)
on structure. Most of the examples are
from the biological realm.*

**"Physics and Size in Biological
Systems"**
Barnes, George
in *The Physics Teacher,* April 1989

*This article gives extensive examples of the
effects of scale on structure. At times, it is
more technical than you may desire, but
you can skip over those bits without losing
the key ideas.*

Audiovisual Materials

Filmstrips

Ancient Monuments and Mysteries
National Geographic Society
Filmstrip (14 minutes) with cassette and
   study guides, $32.95

*Remarkable cave paintings by Ice Age
hunters, Egypt's Great Pyramids, the Nazca
Lines in Peru, Stonehenge, and Minoan ru-
ins on Mediterranean islands are some of
the topics covered in this filmstrip. The nar-
ration discusses their origins, purposes, and
construction.*

Videos

Powers of Ten
(Available from the Exploratorium Store,
   3601 Lyon St., San Francisco, CA
   94123, 1-800-359-9899)

*This video takes you on an adventure in
magnitudes. Starting at a picnic, you are
transported out to the edges of the universe, then back down into the proton of a
carbon atom. This 21-minute video was
made by Charles and Ray Eames, best*

*known for their contributions to architec-
ture, industrial design, and photography.*

3–2-1 CONTACT Series on Architecture

Children's Television Workshop
1 Lincoln Plaza
New York, NY 10023
(212) 595–3456

*This excellent series includes five half-hour
segments on: **Raising the Big Top** (#611),
Home (#612), **Stack It Up** (#613), **Made
to Fit** (#614), and **Light But Strong**
(#615). For a broadcast schedule, contact
the Children's Television Workshop or your
local public broadcasting station. If you
wish to purchase videotapes (if you are unable to tape them yourself when they are
shown on TV), the cost is $26.84 per tape.
Many libraries also have these tapes. For a
comprehensive teachers guide, send $5.00
to Box TG at the above address.*

Why Buildings Stand Up
Six programs, 1/2-inch VHS;
   $25.00/program, $150.00/series; no
   preview policy
The Salvadori Educational Institute
c/o Weidlinger Associates
333 Seventh Ave.
New York, NY 10001
(212) 563–2844

*Based on the book by the same name,
Why Buildings Stand Up is a series of
videotapes in which Dr. Mario Salvadori
explains the fundamental principles of
architectural structures through classroom
demonstrations. Using commonly available
materials, this master teacher and a group
of sixth-graders explore basic structural principles and illustrate their applications to
architecture in the design of buildings, skyscrapers, bridges, and domes. The six programs are: **Loads on Buildings, Equilibrium and Materials, Bridges, Paper
Structures, Children and Math,** and **History of Architecture and Engineering.***

Appendix C: Blank Charts for Mathematics of Scale Activities

The following pages contain sample blank charts which you may copy, modify, or otherwise use to accompany some of the *Mathematics of Scale* activities.

BLANK CUBE GROWTH CHART

Length of Edge (cube length)	Perimeter of Base (cube length)	Area of Base (face)	Area of Total Surface (face)	Volume (sugar cube)

CUBE SHRINKING CHART

Length of Edge (fraction of big cube edge length)	Area of Base (fraction of big cube face area)	Area of Total Surface (fraction of big cube face area)	Volume (fraction of big cube volume)	Total Number of Cubes	Total Surface of all Cubes (in terms of big cube face area)

CYLINDERS CHART

Cylinder #	Height of Cylinder (h)	Diameter of base (d)	Circum-ference of base (c)	Area of base (cm²)	Area of cylinder surface (can surfaces)	Volume (cans)
1						
2						
3						
4						
5						
. . .	. . .	. . .	. . .	. . .	. . .	. . .

CONE CHART

Cone #	Length of cone side (cm)	Height of cone (cm)	Diameter of base (cm)	Circum-ference of base (cm)	Area of base (cm²)	Area of cone surface (cm²)	Volume (little cones)

Name: _____

Name: _____

Date: _____

Fruit and Vegetable Measurement

Name of Fruit or Vegetable: _____

Measure	Small	Large	Large/Small
LINEAR Units _____			
Length			
Height			
Diameter			
Circumference			
AREA Units _____			
Surface			
Cross section			
VOLUME Units _____			

Appendix D: Sample Science Record Sheets

The following are some sample science record sheets that teachers who helped develop this book have used to help their students use records to analyze their work.

Title:

Group Name:	
1.	3.
2.	4.

Questions:

1) What did you do? Explain your activity.

2) What did you observe? What happened?
   What did you learn?

3) What questions do you have?

4) How do you feel about how your
   team worked together?

   a) What did you do well?

   b) What is a goal for next time?

Science Record Sheet

Science Record Sheet

1. *Predict* what you think will happen.

2. *Discuss* your prediction with your partner or group.

3. *Write* your prediction.

_____

_____

4. What did you see happening?

_____

_____

_____

5. What do you think is going on here? Why?

_____

_____

_____

6. What questions do you have?
   ("I wonder. . . ?" "What if. . . ?" "How come. . . ?")

_____

*You may use the back of this sheet to write questions or draw illustrations.

Science Record Sheet

Title: _____ Date: _____

Group Name: _____

1. _____ 3. _____

2. _____ 4. _____

Do the following *before* you begin your activity:

1. *Predict* what you think will happen and hypothesize causes.

2. *Discuss* your prediction and hypotheses with your partner or group.

3. *Write* your prediction and hypotheses:

_____

_____

_____

_____

_____

_____

During the Activity:

1. *Do/Observe* the activity. Take notes, draw, or record data if you choose.

2. *Discuss* what you observe with your partner or group.

(continued next page)

(continued from previous page)

After the Activity:

1. *Discuss* and *answer* the following questions:

    1. What did you use?

_____

_____

    2. What did you do? (explain your activity)

_____

_____

_____

_____

    3. What did you observe? What happened?

_____

_____

_____

_____

    4. Write your hypotheses here. Change it later if you want.

_____

    5. Write at least three things you learned. (You may want to think about generalizations or conclusions.)

1. _____

2. _____

3. _____

(continued next page)

(continued from previous page)

6. What questions do you have? Write at least one "What if. . . ?" question. Use the back of this sheet, if necessary.

_____

_____

_____

7. How do you feel about how your team worked together? What did you do well? What is a goal for next time?

_____

_____

_____

8. You may illustrate your findings below:

***EXTRA CREDIT:

It you were to repeat the experiment, would you do anything differently? If so, describe.

On a separate sheet of paper, design an experiment or investigation to test one or more of your questions.